THE GIRL WH(

The Girl Who Dated Herself

SUSANNAH SHAKESPEARE

COUPER STREET BOOKS

A story that is mostly true...

For FM
(we were on a break)

And
Julie

And
Sharon

Couper Street Books is a publishing brand involved in the professional production
and publication management of books. All rights in and responsibilities for the
contents remain with the author.

001

The line quoted in Chapter 2 is from *Franny and Zooey* by J. D. Salinger.
The references in Chapter 7 are to *Big Red Barn* and *Goodnight Moon*, both by Margaret Wise Brown.
All other quotes, books and songs are credited within the text where they appear.
Any omissions or inaccuracies in the form of credits are unintentional and
corrections may be made to future printings.

The fictional names given to the majority of the characters in this story have been chosen at
random and any similarities to persons living or dead are coincidental and unintentional.

Cover design: Couper Street Books
Typeset by Couper Street Type Company

First published worldwide in 2019

A CIP catalogue record for this book is available from the British Library

ISBN (HB) 978-1-9993477-1-0
ISBN (TPB) 978-1-9993477-6-5
ISBN (ebook) 978-1-9993477-3-4

www.couperstreetbooks.com
www.susannahshakespeare.com

ACKNOWLEDGEMENTS

I would like to thank everyone who helped produce this book, especially Couper Street Books, Dan Prescott and Claire Wingfield. I thank my many friends and family members, especially those who've supported me through the worst of times and celebrated with me at the best of times. My thanks to Jude (whose writing talent continually inspires me) for creating a safe space and encouraging me to share my story. Hugues, Emily, Esther, Pierre and Paul, thank you for giving me a house to write in and a home to bang drums in… I love you all equally. Finally, this book would not exist without the many people who kept urging me to write it… thank you for believing in me and I hope it meets your expectations.

TABLE OF CONTENTS

I'm calling this a memoir, even though I am breaking many rules of the genre. There are plenty of fictional elements in this story. *Almost* all the names and characters mentioned here are made up, but they all play roles that were played, either within the moment I'm describing, or at another time in my life, by real people. So in that sense there is a truth within them all. So why not call this a novel? Because the heart and bones of the book are based on events and experiences that actually happened. The places I describe are, for the most part, absolutely real or based on somewhere real. The journey I will reveal to you is true. The passage of time during which this journey took place is accurate.

It was also, at some point, suggested to me that I classify this as a "self-help" book. But that would impose upon it an importance or *purpose* that I wouldn't feel comfortable with. I'm sharing this story simply because, whenever I've told it, people have urged me to write it. If it does help you, as much as it helped me, that would be a wonderful thing. But ultimately, my only *intention* is to entertain… and perhaps provoke some thoughts about the value of exploring the real truth, which is our own truth.

Susannah Shakespeare
December 2018

"Begin at the beginning," the King said gravely, "And go on till you come to the end: then stop."

Alice's Adventures in Wonderland,
Chapter 12

LEWIS CARROLL

CHAPTER ONE

The Girl Who Made Another Bad Choice

*Men generally invest in a lot of kissing to get
you into bed, not into a relationship...*

"**M**y therapist says I can't date you."
"Your therapist is a celibate gay *priest*!" I pro-
tested.

Only in Los Angeles does a neurotic Jewish sex addict go
to a gay Catholic priest for relationship advice.

"I made a great case for you. I told him you were bitchin'
hot and super smart, but he said I really should stay single
at the moment and work on my codependency issues."

"Your co-de-*what*?!"

This is what you get for believing in love at first sight.

Relationships are all about making choices. Some people
make great choices. Others continually get it wrong. Why?
Was it simply random bad luck that had brought all my
relationships – from the three-week flings to the five-year
marathon – to an end, or was something specific at play
here?

My father's philosophical advice to me, when I was nine-
teen and lying on my bed, weeping inconsolably after the
most recent love of my life turned out to be another frog

once kissed, was: "Why do you get so upset? All relationships end, either through death or divorce. None of them can last forever, so just forget about him and move on to the next one."

"But there isn't anyone else," I'd wailed. "He was *the one*…"

Cut to twenty-three more "ones" later and…

I'd met Zachary (never a Zach) in a park opposite Fox Studios. It wasn't my neighbourhood, I'd never been in this park before, but I'd been sitting in stationary traffic on Pico Boulevard, on my way back from a meeting in Venice Beach, for well over an hour. I was desperate to stretch my legs. So I'd found a parking spot and got out to take a stroll.

I'd been in the park less than five minutes when I noticed a silhouette moving towards me, backlit by the sun, like something emerging from a mirage, aura first. Finally, the shape morphed into a man and his dog. It was a strange-looking dog, with a head far too small for its body. It looked at me suspiciously; the feeling was mutual. But its owner was a vision to behold so I disingenuously made a fuss of the dog.

"Cute dog," I lied, crouching down to pet it.

"He likes you, too," said the dog owner, who was clearly way out of touch with his pet… or was simply trying to impress me, too. "I'm Zachary."

"Jessica," I batted back.

"Generally considered a Jewish name." He made the statement sound like a question. I'd seen many eyes light up in anticipation just like that.

"Indeed. But I'm afraid I'm a fake. It goes way back. On my father's side. I'd still have to convert if we got married."

He laughed. Oh the relief. That line was hit or miss.

"And British," he observed, appreciatively. "I love your accent."

"Yes, of course you do," I sighed, dramatically, making Zachary laugh. "I am aware of the law in your country that states everyone must respond that way when first introduced to a British person. It *sounds* like a compliment but is clearly a hostile strike since *we* spoke the language first and *you* bastardised it, and thus are the culprits of using an *accent*."

He was laughing hard now. Even the dog looked mildly impressed.

But it was always like that when it was love at first sight. It was like I could do nothing wrong, like every line I said was just what the guy wanted to hear. Like every gesture I chose was the right one. Everything unfolding like it was meant to be, leading me to believe that fate had brought us together and that, now we had finally found each other, we would never be apart again. Me never guessing – never, not even for one second – that the guy might be *allowing* me to feel this way, encouraging this magical moment, because he could spot a sucker like me a mile away, and it was a tried and tested tactic to get a girl like me into bed as soon as possible.

It took Zachary less than twenty-four hours.

I was aware of the concept and rules of "casual sex". I'd watched Samantha on *Sex and the City*, in awe and wonder. I *wanted* to be this cool, liberated girl who slept with any guy she wanted, crept out of his apartment at 4am and ended up having to change her number because he just wouldn't stop calling. But I wasn't. I'd start out with good intentions – *I won't even give him my number* – but if I got so much as five seconds of a really good kiss, I was picturing us on our wedding day. I was well aware that this was the result of too many fairy tales as a child and rom coms as a teenager, teaching me that people just found each other – it was their *destiny* – and lived happily ever after. I just didn't know how to stop believing the fantasy.

Not so long before this moment (meeting Zachary in the park) I'd believed, with every fibre of my being, that there would never be another moment like this again because I was *with* the man who was my destiny. Or so I thought. It wasn't perfect, but it had been five years, we loved each other, I assumed we'd get married. No alternative future entered my mind. But six months ago, even *that* prince turned into a frog and broke my heart.

Being at the age when society and the media and your mother collectively scream down a megaphone, "OH MY GOD, FIND A MAN IMMEDIATELY! YOU HAVE NO TIME TO LOSE. IF YOU DON'T HAVE CHILDREN, YOU WILL REGRET IT FOREVER. YOUR LIFE WILL BE WASTED," I panicked. When my body chimed in with, "I AM NOT WAITING FOREVER! WE ARE WASTING ANOTHER EGG EVERY MONTH. THE CLOCK IS TICKING!" I ran, like a banshee, to the nearest bar I could find.

Yes, two weeks after coming out of a five-year relationship I found myself in a bar, on St. Patrick's Day, looking for my baby daddy.

For some reason that I've never quite worked out, for one night of the year, and one night only, the whole of Los

Angeles gets absolutely wasted. There are plenty of other celebratory nights but none seem to be as all-inclusive and all-alcohol-consuming as St. Paddy's Day.

It's also the night on which L.A. residents are prepared to look most ridiculous.

In general, people take their costumes pretty seriously in L.A. There are too many talented, artistic people around, with too much time on their hands. If you want to see what I mean, go hang out in West Hollywood and watch the Halloween Parade along Santa Monica Boulevard... it's spectacular. But on March the 17th every year, the cheapest, stupidest floppy top hats and green socks come out. T-shirts with terrible slogans are worn ("I'm so Irish my liver hates me" is *not* funny) as the whole town comes out in celebration of good old binge drinking and hard-core alcoholism.

So it's not too hard to get laid.

If you've a pulse, you'll have the luck of the Irish.

And that's the attitude with which I entered Molly Malone's on Fairfax that night.

It only took me two circuits of the bar to find him. He was giving me that "I'm noticing you noticing me noticing you" look. I positioned myself at the bar, five bodies and ten pints of Guinness between us, and waited to get served. We watched each other, in silent agreement that we were in competition to get the bartender's attention first. He won and ordered four pints of Guinness. He weaved his way through the crowd and gave me two of them.

So, two pints (at least) and several shots of Jameson's later, and we were back at his place, tearing each other's clothes off.

★

The problem with spending five years in a relationship with a particularly well-endowed man (even if he wasn't too adept at using it) is that you kind of lose your sense of perspective.

I didn't mean to freeze in horror as I closed my hand around what could only be described as a baby carrot.

There's that awful, awkward moment at a time like this, when you *really* hope that you didn't stifle a laugh, that no exclamatory noise emerged from your mouth, but the reaction of the person you're with kind of indicates otherwise.

I can only describe what happened as "immediate detumescence".

I tried everything I could think of to recover tumescence, but to no avail. Finally he rolled away from me.

"I guess you're just not attractive enough to me," he mumbled. Making it clear that it was my fault he couldn't get it up.

I got dressed and drove home sobbing, believing that the humiliation was all mine.

So now I had managed to get dumped by the love of my life *and* fail to re-erect a tiny penis within a couple of weeks.

What a loser!

But back to Zach(ary).

Zachary was a composer. He wrote incidental music, mostly for bad TV movies, but he was a classically trained musician. He told me that he had a Kawai baby grand (genuinely my favourite piano in the world) at home. He lived on the other side of the park.

Like, wouldn't *you* believe that this was "meant to be"?

He had credits. He was on IMDb. It was Hollywood; we probably knew some of the same people, at least people within a degree or two of separation. Of course it was safe to go to his house... on a "he's probably not going to murder me" level, perhaps not a hygiene level. But I overlooked the mess, the filth, and the smell of mould in his dark and dank one-bedroom apartment. If this was "meant to be", none of the details mattered. He lived in a characterless, two-storey building on Beverly Drive in an area real estate agents like to call "Beverly Hill Adjacent" despite the fact that it's around 20 blocks from the city limit.

I kind of floated over to the piano and sat down. It had been a while, I was out of practice, but I knew what would impress him.

I half flew and half butchered my way through Ludwig van Beethoven's Piano Sonata No. 8 in C minor, Op. 13 (commonly known as *Sonata Pathétique*). It was the first time I'd played the piece in well over a year. It didn't go too badly; it was full of wrong notes and painful hesitations, but I got through it, and some sections sounded rather good. It made me want to find somewhere to practice again.

I sent him a text later that night saying, *you make me want to be a better pianist*.

As I lifted my fingers off the keys after the final, long-held chord, his fingers were on my shoulders. He was kneeling beside the piano stool, telling me I'd played beautifully, telling me *I* was beautiful, running his fingers up the back of my neck and into my hair, holding my head, firmly but gently, and pulling my face towards him, staring into my eyes.

Such intense feelings came up. It had been six months since I'd been touched or looked at like this by anyone. I honestly thought no one would ever want me again because I had been so wrecked by rejection. In the eyes that locked onto mine… I saw hope. (Or rather, I *projected* hope.) And then he was kissing me.

I just fell apart. Literally. I actually burst into tears and had to push him away.

"Oh my god, I am so sorry," I blurted out. "I'm so embarrassed. It's just… this is too much. I'm overwhelmed."

"I know," he said, gently.

"I have to go. But you have my number." We'd exchanged numbers in the park because he'd asked if he could take me for coffee one day. That was just before he'd lured me to his lair with the promise of a go on his piano.

He was messaging me before I got back to my car. *I have to see you again soon.* No guy messaged me so soon after meeting. They all played the game… followed the golden rule… waited at least two days. *Will you come over tonight?* My heart was racing. *Just to talk. I promise. I just need to be with you.* Obviously I felt the same.

I went home, showered, changed, sent excited text messages to my closest girlfriends declaring – *It just feels like it was meant to be, like I have finally found the one* – and drove back to Zachary's.

True to his word, he didn't try anything. But by 4am I wanted him so badly I made all the moves. I had completely fallen in love with his talent. He had showed me his studio and I had melted. I don't know why I find synthesizers so sexy. Maybe because I'm in awe of all the magical things they can do.

We'd only been drinking tea but I was drunk on love. I

devoured him. And he devoured me. And the kissing was *great*. And the rest of it was *great*. And finally we were in his bed and every single thing that was a little weird and disgusting about his apartment escaped me…

Until something got in the way that I simply couldn't ignore.

Look, I don't know where you stand on having dogs in beds and I'm not judging you, but I don't do it. They don't go on the bed when it's empty, they don't go on the bed when I'm sleeping in it, and they *definitely* don't go on the bed when I'm having sex in it.

The dog had been skittish around me since we met; it now turned aggressively pushy. We had a serious territory issue going on. Every time Zachary and I got into a groove, the dog would stick its nose where no dog's nose should *ever* go. I gently nudged it off the bed… three times.

Finally, I suggested that we should put the dog outside the room and shut the door. Zachary looked at me oddly.

"That's not very kind."

I made a joke about not really being into threesomes, of the human or bestial kind, but that went down like the proverbial lead balloon, so I straight up said, "It's just that I'm finding it a bit uncomfortable with him getting on the bed with us."

Zachary narrowed his eyes at me, coldly, "But it's his bed, too."

I got my way (presumably because, at that point I offered Zachary more than the dog could… at least I *hope* that was the case) but he must have let the dog in again when I was sleeping because I woke up at 10am to find myself curled up awkwardly in the corner of the bed. Zachary was spooning the dog. I got dressed and gently nudged Zachary awake.

"I have to go. I have a meeting. I'll call you later. Shall I come over tonight?"

"Hmm? Um, no." His eyes were still closed. "Sorry, doll, I have a date tonight."

What?!

"What kind of date?"

"A date date."

"I'm confused."

He opened his eyes finally and looked up at me, and snuggled a little closer to the dog.

"Hey, doll, you know, we had a great time but I'm not looking to commit to anyone at the moment."

"Sure," I said, completely unsure.

I will confess right now, I have had a long history of not managing my expectations when it comes to boys. When I was 12, I made the assumption that the 14-year-old boy I had shared my first kiss with was henceforth my boy-friend… soon to be fiancé.

"A kiss is not a contract," my older, more experienced (she'd been fingered) friend had to explain to me. I'd done my best to remember and accept that men generally invest in a lot of kissing to get you into bed, not into a relationship. But what Zachary and I done the night before was a *lot* more than kissing.

As his dog is my witness.

My eyes were *aching* with the effort of holding back the tears, but I firmly believed one should not cry in front of a boy more than once in a twenty-four-hour period. I started to get up off the bed, but he grabbed my hand – and not in the tender way I remembered him touching me the night before.

"Look, doll, I know you're upset but it's not you, it's me." *Oh shoot me in the head, NOW!* "The truth is, I'm a sex addict. Monogamy doesn't work for me. I don't want to hurt you. It wouldn't be fair to you, you know, to get too involved with me."

I couldn't speak because I was biting the inside of my cheek. So he carried on, continuing to squeeze my hand in an oddly possessive way.

"But here's the thing, doll. I think you rock and I want you in my life. I want to be close to you. Can we do that? Can we just hang out and be close and get to know each other? No strings attached? I'd really like it if we could do that. Can we?"

Now this may sound like a perfectly reasonable request to you. You may have even been in his shoes (or underpants) and found yourself saying something similar to someone. But the point here is this: I did *not* want to hang out with the man who had just broken my heart because I'd mistaken his carnal desire for some kind of beautiful connection that *meant* something. I did *not* want to be a girl he could occasionally sleep with; one of several girls he was occasionally sleeping with. I did not want that at all. However, because I assumed I was in love with him and meant to be with him, and was convinced he was in love with me, too, and would soon realize it, I said,

"Okay," kissed him, and left.

And cried all the way home.

*

He proceeded to call me three times a day. Minimum. Each time, we spoke for an hour or more. We played online Scrabble, jazzed by the discovery we were very well matched in skill level. It was Yom Kippur so we didn't see each other for a few days while he busied himself with fasting and atoning, and amusing me with anecdotes about the inappropriate comments his mother made at temple. He was slightly obsessed with his mother; he talked about her a *lot*. He got sick (I've never believed all that fasting is good for you) and asked me to pick up chicken soup for him and bring it round. I did, but he didn't want me to come *inside* the house and get infected, so we walked around the block twice… with the dog, of course, who kept looking at me triumphantly.

In two weeks it felt like we'd had more conversations than I'd had with my ex over the course of five years. It was like our brains had fused together. I was in deep. Although something was off. Once he'd gotten over his cold, there was plenty of hugging and handholding… but no kissing.

He was a sex addict who didn't want to sleep with me. (And I thought rejection by a mini wiener felt bad!)

There were endless emails and text messages. And the epic phone calls continued. If he *was* sleeping with anyone else I would have been impressed that he managed to fit it in between our phone calls. Maybe he could text and fuck simultaneously.

It all came to a head, literally, on my birthday.

I invited him to come to dinner with some friends of mine. He asked me to come over first. It was the first time I'd actually been inside the apartment since the first time. The dog wasn't impressed. Zachary presented me with a very odd collection of poorly wrapped gifts. A VHS tape of Blackadder (I didn't even know anyone with a VHS player; I'd seen one in a museum somewhere a few years before), a plant pot without a plant in it, and a notebook with the first five pages ripped out.

I'd tuned out from the deafening cacophony of alarm bells by then, so I didn't even flinch when he asked me to give him a few minutes to make himself something to eat *before* we went to dinner.

I drove us to the little pizza place near The Grove, ignoring the little voice in my head saying, "And why isn't he offering to drive so that you can have a drink?" He didn't like to drive. I had already ignored the voice complaining that, "Those gifts were crap he'd found lying around, probably in his mother's house. And has he ever even bought you a coffee?" And I certainly wasn't answering the voice demanding to know, "Are you his friend, his girlfriend, his lover or his therapist?" (The last one, at least, for sure.) But I didn't mind, I had dated so many repressed men that it was *refreshing* to spend time with someone who found it so easy to talk about themselves... 24 hours a day... *every* day.

It was a very strange and stilted evening. My friends were already not on board with this man who had monopolised my time and was giving me nothing in return. He ordered the cheapest beer on the menu, didn't eat anything, and when the check came, asked if I'd include the beer in my share... at the same time that my friends offered to absorb my share and split it, so that I didn't have to pay anything on my birthday. They looked pointedly at Zachary after announcing this but he said nothing. In fact, he seemed like he was sulking. He'd been awkward since the moment we arrived, behaving like a possessive boyfriend, clasping my hand in his all night, staring at me, making no effort to engage with my friends and even interrupting them in order to get my attention, usually to say something pretty random and mundane.

As I drove him back to his place, he continued to act like a moody teenager, answering me in nonchalant, mono-syllabic grunts every time I tried to start a conversation.

Finally, we got back to his place and I pulled up, cut the engine and turned to him. He was staring out of the window.

"What's wrong? You've been down all night."

"It's obvious your friends don't like me," he whined, still not looking at me. I suppressed a laugh.

"To be sure, they don't know you," I quipped, in a less-than-mediocre Irish accent. He didn't laugh. But a moment later he turned to face me with a stupid grin on his face.

"You know what would make me feel better…"

I noticed he was fumbling with his pants. I lowered my eyes slowly.

One part of his anatomy was most certainly *not* feeling down.

Don't judge me for not kicking him out of the car. I'm a people pleaser.

His cousin was staying so he said he couldn't invite me in when I asked. He said he'd call me the next day… after therapy.

I drove home alone pleased that there had finally been some kissing… at least by me, and sort of part of him. Now (I assumed) we could move our relationship forward.

Which brings us neatly to the moment when I was

informed that his gay Catholic priest/therapist was not sanctioning such a move.

"But I thought we weren't dating anyway," I argued weakly, "You said we were just hanging out… being friends."

"Oh, doll, let's not pretend. You sucked my dick last night. My friends don't suck my dick." (He called his mother doll: another red flag I'd ignored.)

Humiliated, I cradled the phone in both hands, thankful that he could not see my face, with the tears running down my cheeks, trying to comprehend how I was getting dumped from a relationship I was not actually in.

"So what now?" I asked in a very small voice.

"Bad news, I'm afraid," he said gravely, as if announcing a fatality. "We have to have a clean break. I can't see you anymore."

I thought I was going to throw up so I got out of my car, which I had pulled over to the side of the road in order to take his call. I sat down under a tree and did a quick survey of my surroundings, in case I needed to expel the previous night's pizza from my guts in a hurry.

"Look," he sighed. *Oh, don't say it, PLEASE don't say it. Anything but—* "It's not you. It's me." I wished it was my death he was sombrely announcing. "I promise you that, doll. I'm sorry, but I can't see you anymore, or have any contact with you at all. Please respect my wishes on this. I have to work on my issues and the only way I can do that is by completely removing myself from your presence. You rock, you really do, but I can't have any contact with you right now. So I must ask you to respect my wishes and not contact me at all."

But you were the one who initiated this obsessive non-stop

17

contact in the first place, I wanted to shout. But I didn't. I didn't say anything.

From somewhere I found the strength to hang up. Goodbye. *Zach*.

Out of spite (because I'd really cut back for him as he hated it) I chain-smoked three cigarettes. And that's how we find me sitting on the sidewalk on a tree-lined residential street in Los Feliz sobbing my heart out between drags.

I wasn't that conscious of my actions, but I was probably wailing loudly, and rocking back and forth trying to hold myself together, by the time a white Subaru Outback stopped in the middle of the street. The window rolled down and the warm face of a large, middle-aged Hispanic woman stared at me with grave concern.

"Señorita, Policía? You need? I call?" She waved her cell phone at me. I took a deep breath and shook my head.

"No, no, it's okay..." I managed without choking. "It's nothing. It's just a guy. Un hombre. He crush me. My heart..." I mimed ripping my heart from my chest, throwing it on the floor and stamping on it. It was a very convincing mime. I felt the pain.

The kind señora's face softened. She gave me such a heartfelt look of sympathy that it set me off again. I let out an embarrassingly loud high-pitched noise as more tears sprung from my eyes. My new friend rolled her eyes and shook her head.

"He no good for you, chica," she called out. "You make bad choice. You fix *this*," she said, pointing to her head. "And then it will fix *this*." She placed her hand on her ample left bosom, indicating her heart.

And something in that gesture brought about a sudden hiatus in my tantrum. I became still and silent as I stared at her. *What? You mean this is all my fault? But I can fix it?*

"You gonna be okay. I know," she reassured me, with a smile. She patted her head, then her heart, one more time, then drove off.

I stared after the Subaru as it indicated left and turned up the next street. Was it possible that when Zach had said, "It's not you, it's me," he was wholly mistaken? Was it my choices alone that had brought me here, sitting on my butt, on this sidewalk, crying over a man who'd been in my life for little more than a month?

I'd been here before. Not on this particular sidewalk, but I'd been here emotionally... *so* many times. I'd been getting my heart broken on a regular basis since I was seven years old. And what (or rather who) was the common denominator in *every* single scenario?

Me.

It wasn't a comfortable feeling, coming to the realization that I had brought all that pain on myself, that I was responsible in some way for every horrible feeling I'd experienced. But there was hope in the Subaru lady's words.

Because if I *had* been causing it all, she was right... only I had the power to fix it.

At that point I had no idea how, but the very notion gave me a glimmer of hope.

"Who in the world am I? Ah, THAT'S the great puzzle!"

Alice's Adventures in Wonderland,
Chapter 2

LEWIS CARROLL

The Girl Who Quit Smoking

I wasn't smoking them; they were smoking me.

L et's take a little snapshot of my life at this exact point. This was the third time I'd ended up setting up camp in Los Angeles for work. The first two times I'd been hired by mid-level production companies to research and develop material from other writers. Somewhat unimpressed by the material I received (there was plenty of good stuff out there but it all went to the big producers, none of it came our way), I'd started writing a bit myself. A fledgling company that had made it big off the strength of a star client's TV show was intending to produce a television show I'd created. Until they got the green light from the network we were "in development". They would send me notes now and again, I'd do a rewrite, and they'd say the network was still considering it. This had been going on for a year.

Initially there had been great excitement about this show. One producer, upon reading my first draft, had said, "You know, this is an *Emmy-winning* show right here. You better not forget to thank me in your acceptance speech." There was a big, fancy director attached, who had an office at Fox Studios. I'd been taken from the parking lot to my first meeting with him in a golf buggy, like in the movies. It had all been really exciting. But nothing had actually *happened* and it felt like we were going around in circles.

"We just have one last round of notes for you and then we think it's a go," I'd been told five times already.

You already know that my five-year relationship didn't survive its transformation into a long-distance one. Truth was, it shouldn't have survived past a six-month whirlwind romance, but I was a Class A Clinger and I had let it drag on well past its sell-by date. The added pressure of trying to do it long-distance for a year had simply been the final nail in the coffin.

Friendships in Los Angeles can be pretty ephemeral and I had recently discovered that some of the people I thought I was close to, who I'd known from my first and second L.A. incarnations, had disappeared from my life. They'd moved up the Hollywood food chain and left me behind. This happens to us all. I'd reassured myself that they were "not real friends" anyway and doubled up efforts with the few friends I still had.

My patience – after a year in "development hell" – was wearing thin and I was constantly on the verge of telling the production company where to shove their *Emmy-award winning show*, but I had read *Franny and Zoey* and knew that "You can't just walk out on the results of your own hankerings." That would be tantamount to artistic sacrilege. "Cause and effect, buddy, cause and effect."

Hmm, it seemed to me that my "cause" was to have come up with the hare-brained notion that I could be a successful TV writer. The "effect" was a lot of waiting around and broken promises, and endless days filled with frustration and disappointment. They had really built me up, those producers, making me believe that fame and fortune were just around the corner. That's what they do. And the months roll by and you finally realize the phone just isn't ringing any more… and that you are officially a Nobody.

The worst place on earth to be a Nobody is Hollywood. The place is so full of Nobodies, you can't even stand out for your Nobodiness; you're just one Nobody in a sea of a million Nobodies. People move to L.A. – from Texas to Nebraska, from Toronto to Vancouver, from London to Rome, and from Cape Town to Perth – because they want to become a *Somebody*. And if they can't be a Somebody, they will settle for being an *Anybody*. They may have arrived wanting to be an actor and ended up being a casting director; they may have arrived with visions of becoming the next Spielberg but ended up running a studio; they may have come to design film sets and ended up designing multi-million dollar Malibu homes. The point is, *everyone* originally moved to Hollywood because they wanted to be a star. They came with their acceptance speeches on the tips of their tongues and their autobiographies half written on their laptops.

But it wasn't fame they needed; it was *validation*. They just wanted to be recognised, by their peers, and their audience, for their art… their life's work. So when they don't get the validation, they grab hold of anything to soothe the pain. Because they worked and worked, and created *so much* art… but the big break never came, except for the one in their hearts. The true American dream – that says you can be anything if you work hard and long enough at it – is only sustainable for a finite amount of people. In Hollywood, unfortunately, it is just over-subscribed.

*

"I always wanted to be a stand-up comedian but I was afraid people would laugh at me." Well, it made me laugh. And I think one of the five people in the audience smiled.

The ultimate sanctuary for real Hollywood Nobodies is the Open Mic night; partly because it's free therapy. You are guaranteed attention for ten minutes or so. You get to *stand in the spotlight*, just for writing your name down on a list and paying $5 on the door.

And it's not actually as desperate as it sounds; it's actually quite a smart move. You see, comedy is the ultimate meritocracy. You can show up, no job, no agent, no credits, no friends, and if people laugh at you, you have value. If you keep doing well, you get invited to be in a showcase, and from there, you get to perform at bigger clubs.

And *then* you get noticed.

In comedy, no one ever has enough good material. There's always room for a new voice in the writers' room. When the agents can't deliver, the casting directors go to the comedy clubs.

And you can keep going and trying forever. You can be shit for two years, performing to a silent room every Monday night in a dive bar in Toluca Lake, and then suddenly figure out some really good material and it's… *taxi for the man in green leather pants… direct to the Laugh Factory, please.*

No one cares what you look like, or who you know, or where you've come from, or how old you are, or whether you have one wooden leg and no left breast. They will forget that you have sucked for the last ten months if… *you make them laugh tonight!*

I did open mic about five times… before I realized that I really was only doing it for the free therapy.

*

I performed my swansong the night after my birthday; it had been on the calendar for a while. Zach had even promised to come, before his phone call that morning.

If there's one thing I'm known for, it's my tenacity. I am not a quitter, even when the whole world is screaming at me: *QUIT!* I should have cancelled and stayed in bed, nursing my aching heart, but no… masochist that I am, off I went to the little room above a little bar on Gower, near the Hollywood Forever Cemetery.

In case you've a mind to try it, here are the rules when you're on stage, doing a stand-up routine, in a comedy club, anywhere in the world really…

Spilling your guts out about the demise of your relationship is okay.

Telling tales on your kleptomaniac aunt is okay.

Divulging details of your failed attempts to try new sex acts is okay.

Actual crying is *not* okay!

I left before my time was up and hurried out. I decided to drive up to Nichols Canyon, where Greg, my beautiful, gay osteopath was housesitting. He would love this.

You do so much driving in L.A. that if you don't get a good osteopath, you'll end up a cripple. Greg was the best, in my opinion. I recommended him to everyone. He had a network of extremely wealthy friends / clients who he house and pet sat for. He was in high demand. I'm not sure if Greg even had his own place or paid rent anywhere (he was usually paid for housesitting duties, too.) These glamorous houses also provided great locations for trysts with an endless stream of gorgeous young men. If he didn't find what he was looking for in the West Hollywood clubs, he would find it online.

He dated kind of like how I shopped.

The best thing about Greg was that he *loved* drama. He couldn't get enough of it. My impression of James Van Der Beek's ugly cry fest in *Dawson's Creek* may not have impressed the comedy club audience, but I knew Greg would lap it up. In fact, in order to save the best tears for him, I tried to stop myself from crying too much in the car.

So what happened next was definitely not my fault.

Let's take a moment here to talk about me and cars.

I am not a car person.

I am so much *not* a car person I've been known to try to run a car without oil, gas and water, blaming the warning lights for not *actually* speaking to me, even though they've been blinking at me for days. Whenever the basic requirements for car maintenance are explained to me, I zone out. I resent every penny that has to be spent on these polluting contraptions. I like public transport, and taxis for late nights and special occasions. By rights I belong in cities where a car is completely unnecessary, like New York and Paris. But I have spent a good deal of my adult life living in Los Angeles, where not having a car limits your movements too much.

So, because I am really not a car person, I have never cared what my cars look like.

On my first two incarnations I'd leased reasonably nice, but suitably boring, Ford Contours. The first was silver; the second was "champagne" (basically grey, just two shades darker and duller than the silver).

When I arrived for my third incarnation, I was on a budget and decided it would be best to buy a reasonably priced second-hand vehicle for around $1,000, promising myself that I would get it serviced regularly. I picked up what I thought was a real bargain: a '97 Saturn Sedan in gold. I bought it from a mechanic who worked at the auto repair shop behind the Mobil gas station at the corner of Santa Monica and Vine. I called it my "little old lady car" because one friend, laughing at it, said it was the exact same car that her grandmother, in Little Rock, drove.

The Saturn had two rather inconvenient little quirks that I (kind of) grew to live with. The most troublesome, because I would so often forget about it, was the fact that the headlights switch was under the left side of the steering shaft and I regularly hit it with my knee when I was getting out of the car. So I would accidently switch on the headlights (which I wouldn't see if it was broad daylight) and if I happened to be away from the car for any length of time, the battery would die. I'd have to call AAA (who only give you a limited number of free call-outs for this) or stalk other drivers returning to nearby parked vehicles, with my fingers crossed in the hope that they'd have the necessary cables and could give me a jump start.

Naturally this only happened when I was running late or had an urgent meeting somewhere.

The other defining peculiarity about this particular automobile was the fact that the gear selector (it was an automatic vehicle) would occasionally, and totally randomly, get stuck in the "Park" position, and no amount of pushing and shoving would get it to move to "Drive". There were about two occasions when I somehow managed to free it but otherwise it was another call to Triple A.

The only solution to this bizarre problem was to leave the car in "Neutral", obviously ensuring that the parking break was firmly on. For this reason, I was very wary of valet services. No matter how much I urged them to leave the car in "Neutral" when they parked it, explaining that the parking brake would suffice, they would overrule me and put it into "Park". I even balled up some sticky tape and inserted it into the gap so that it was almost impossible to get the car into "Park", but invariably they would shove that baby right out of the way and force that gear selector into the "Park" position. I took to avoiding valet parking wherever possible. Twice, in locations where they had told me it was compulsory, I had offered them a tip to let me park the car.

Nevertheless, I had grown fond of that little car; it had seen me through the best of times and the worst of times, and I never would have let anything hurt it… as long as I stayed of sound mind.

If you've never been in a vehicle when it's collided with another vehicle, if you've never experienced that feeling of total vulnerability when metal hits metal, and you are flung forward, then backward, your heart leaping into your throat, your stomach flipping over, and your life flashing before your eyes, then I assure you, it is not something you can imagine, and I hope you are spared the experience. Because no matter how minor the collision, it is terrifying.

You suddenly become startlingly aware of how powerful these machines, that we take for granted as we go about our daily lives, really are. You get a shocking reminder that if they were to collide at a speed fast enough, they would destroy each other, and any bodies inside them.

★

The accident wasn't technically my fault, although I do believe that, had my reflexes not been compromised, I might have stopped in time or swerved enough to avoid it completely.

I was traveling, at the correct speed, north, up Cahuenga Boulevard. I'd just gone under the 101 Freeway, where the road bends to the left and goes up a little hill. At the crest of the hill, a young kid who (we later found out) had borrowed his mother's car without permission, was waiting to make a left turn out of a side street and travel south on Cahuenga. In order to do this, he obviously had to cross my lane of traffic. At some point, he thought the road was clear and shot out of the side road… just as I was coming over the hill. He saw me and stopped immediately in the middle of the road. This probably saved him some significant injuries and reduced the damage done to his mother's car, because when I swerved and slammed on my brakes, I managed to miss the driver's door and slide into the front left panel of his car.

I was unhurt, apart from being extremely shaken up.

But what happened next changed my life.

In the seconds after the impact I sat, motionless, in my seat, coming to terms with the fact that I was alive and not dead. And then I reached for a cigarette.

My next thought after, "Holy shit, I'm alive!" was, "I must fill my lungs with noxious tar immediately!"

It was completely impulsive. I didn't think, Am I okay… are they okay… are there any witnesses? No, I thought, I *must* have a cigarette. Not "want" a cigarette, but I *must* have one.

I wasn't smoking them; they were smoking me.

*

Several hours later, after insurance details had been exchanged, a witness had given me her number, and I'd reached my destination at the top of Nichols Canyon, the significance of my actions finally hit me. My instincts had saved my life, and my addiction was trying to end it. I wasn't just a smoker; I was an addict. It was a psychological condition. I was not controlling cigarettes; cigarettes were controlling me. It didn't matter what I was doing, or where I was, I was never without that nagging little voice in my head asking when I could have my next smoke break.

To be honest, it had been getting increasingly difficult to negotiate this filthy little habit in the preceding months. Zach's revulsion to it had been an incentive to cut down. And I'd had a thought-provoking experience at a party.

With fabulous weather year round, most L.A. parties are held outside, at least partially so. However, you could never take it for read that you could smoke, even outdoors, when you were on someone else's property.

A few months before I met Zach, I'd been at a party to celebrate the birthday of a friend of a friend. I didn't know many people there; in fact, most of them were out of my Hollywood league and rather intimidating. My insecurity had given even more urgency to my gnawing cravings so I went in search of the hostess, to ask if I could smoke in the back yard.

The lady of the house flashed her million-dollar smile (literally – she was a one-time actress who'd made a fortune doing toothpaste commercials and had opened a chain of vegan restaurants with the residuals) at me.

"*I* don't mind," she said, softly, "But would you mind

going *behind* the gazebo as it really bugs my husband. I'll bring you an ashtray."

And then she laid her hand on my arm, almost protectively, or perhaps sympathetically, and said, "I don't judge you, I smoked for years. But it's not exactly an act of self-love is it?"

The way she said this struck me as odd; it was as if we'd been mid-conversation, talking about acts of self-love, as if she'd answered a question I hadn't asked. As far as I remembered, we'd never discussed self-love; we'd had two short conversations on the two (this night included) occasions we'd ever met. One was the current one, and the previous was about the best ways to dehydrate kale.

Her words came back to me as I sat outside the Nichols Canyon property (a property I most definitely could *not* smoke within). What is smoking an act of then? What *was* the point of these expensive, foul-smelling instruments of death and destruction? And what made me compulsively put them between my lips at regular intervals, with no good purpose... no definable reason?

The strength of the addiction finally hit me. I was completely powerless over these stupid, pointless, paper-wrapped sticks of tobacco. And for that reason, and that reason only – not because of the health risks, the cost, the inconvenience of finding anywhere where it was socially acceptable to smoke in L.A., but because I was a control freak and couldn't accept something having such a hold over me – I realized they had to go.

And I knew they had to go for good.

I was about to break up with the *real* love of my life.

*

I picked up my open pack of American Spirit Yellows from where it lay on the passenger seat beside me, and retrieved the emergency pack from the glove box. I hunted through my bag to find every lighter and box of matches. I got out of the car and opened the trunk, where I took the half-full carton (it had four packs left in it) out of the trunk. I walked across the street and threw the whole lot into the big black garbage can that was sitting outside the house.

I took a deep breath and then walked up to the front door and rang the doorbell. When Greg answered, I stared at him, my eyes filling with tears, suddenly aware that I was shaking from head to toe, and said, "I had a car accident. And I quit smoking."

He took me in and gave me brandy.

The first 72 hours went well. I went cold turkey. I found suitable substitutes. I downed the best part of a bottle of red wine each night, ate my own body weight in potato chips (I constantly craved fat and salt), transferred my addiction to Red Vines and cherry Chupa Chups, which I sucked on permanently, and bought a small tapestry so that I had something to do with my hands.

I stopped short of leaving leaflets displaying my photo and the words "DO NOT SELL THIS GIRL CIGARETTES" at all the liquor stores and gas stations in a three-mile radius. The idea went through my head several times.

As I got to the end of the third day, I thought I was over the worst… but then, on that third night, I got hit by what felt like a thunderbolt.

Basically there was a monster that had been living inside me and he was in an almighty rage. His name was

My Nicotine Addiction. Starved of his drug, he'd been sulking for three days, keeping a low profile, waiting to see if I was really serious. He held out hope for a while. He was sure I'd cave. After three days, when he realized there was no more nicotine, not now, not ever, he went ballistic.

I had never experienced rage like it. My entire body felt as though it was on fire. I started crying uncontrollably and gnashing my teeth. I wanted to bite something. I didn't even want food; I wanted to sink my teeth into something that would fight back. I tried biting my arm, but it was too soft, so I shoved my fist into my mouth, which helped muffle the sound of me howling like a wounded wolf. I lay on the floor beating the ground with my hands and feet, like a two-year-old having a tantrum.

Suddenly I needed to move. I jumped up and marched up and down on the spot, stamping my feet. Then I went for a run. I had never been for a run in my life. Finally, I ran a scolding hot bath and got in it so quickly that I almost boiled myself alive. I submerged my whole body, lying face down, and held my head under water until I really thought I might black out. When my chest began to hurt, I finally lifted my head out of the water and gasped for breath.

I lay on my bed and wrapped every blanket I could find around me, burying myself in the covers. Then I curled up into the smallest ball possible and cried myself to sleep.

The rage abated but I was weepy all the next day. I was bereft. Life had become unrecognizable. I had been rejected by, or had rejected, everything that had ever given me love (or what I called love, if a dysfunctional, narcissistic boyfriend or the risk of lung cancer could be construed as love).

I drove down to the beach, because looking at the ocean usually made me feel better. I found an unexpired meter on 4th Street just north of Ocean Park Boulevard. Such good parking karma would usually make me feel particularly lucky and happy, but when I switched off the car, I started crying again. At first it was a light sob, but as the thoughts circled around my head, it became an outpouring, like the tears couldn't leave my eyes fast enough. I cried with despair, as if I was grieving for more than I was even aware of having lost. Something was leaving me forever, I felt. I didn't even know what it was but I didn't want to let go. I felt like I was sinking, being pushed down by a huge weight, and I had no strength to fight it.

How had I ended up here? Not here, in Santa Monica, physically (I'd taken the 101 to the 110 to the 10 and got off at Lincoln to get here)… I mean here in *life*? I hadn't asked for much, had I? Just for someone to love… who would love me back. Why did they all leave?

I'd had so many dreams. I had imagined such a wonderful life. I'd worked so hard. I had done my best to do everything right, so why had everything gone wrong? I felt like I was lost in a maze. I thought I knew where I was going but I'd forgotten the way. I couldn't get out. There was no one there to ask for help. I was all on my own.

Before I slipped into a state of total self-pity, I reminded myself – as I often did – of that scene in *Arthur* (the original, of course), when John Gielgud (as the butler, Hobson) slaps Dudley Moore (as Arthur) around the face after the drunken millionaire finishes a self-pitying rant.

"You feel unloved?" Gielgud asks, rhetorically. "Well, welcome to the world. Everyone is unloved. Now stop feeling sorry for yourself. And incidentally, I love you."

But on this occasion it made me feel sadder than ever.

I didn't even have a Hobson who loved me.

I managed to stop crying and when I was more composed, I got out of the car, took in a few long breaths of sea air, and set off towards the beach. When I reached it I took my shoes off and walked barefoot across the warm sand; there's plenty of it on Santa Monica beach, it's a fair way from the bike path that runs between the road and the beach down to the water's edge.

With all that space, there's room for everyone. Along the bike path you have the walkers, the runners, the rollerbladers... and beside them the parents with strollers and the wheelchair users. Along the beach there are volleyball courts, monkey bars, kids' playgrounds. Down towards the water you get the drum circles, and then the sunbathers, and the surfers preparing their gear, and... the yogis. Or whatever you call people who meditate.

On this occasion, I walked past three people sitting on the sand in what I believed (although it had been a long time since my last yoga class so I couldn't swear to it) was known as the lotus position.

I wasn't entirely sure what meditating was. I'd enjoyed the quiet time at the end of the few yoga classes I'd been to, but I generally used it to run through a shopping list, or try to remember who amongst my friends and family next had a birthday coming up. These people looked like pros. They were just sitting still on the beach.

And I noticed something else. They were all smiling.

I got a few feet from the water's edge and sat down.

Well, I resolved after a minute or two, it couldn't hurt to try, could it?

Whenever I had to wing something in life, I copied. I had seen how these people sat, so I crossed my legs under myself and sat like that. I touched my middle fingers to my thumbs to make little circles, like I'd seen them doing, and rested the back of my hands on my knees. I straightened my back so I looked as though I had very good deportment and closed my eyes. Oh, I nearly forgot... then I smiled.

After about two minutes I thought to myself, Well, I don't know what they've got to smile about, *this is bloody uncomfortable*. I wiggled my butt around in the sand a little, rolled my shoulders, stretched my neck from side to side and tried to settle myself.

A sudden gust of wind blew my hair into my mouth and sand up my nose. I was very close to packing it in.

Okay, I decided, wiggling a bit again, I'd have one more go.

Third time lucky.

I settled myself and started taking some deep breaths, counting as I breathed in and out, as I suddenly remembered we'd been taught to do in yoga.

My deepest thoughts were suddenly in front of me as clear as day... the words almost emblazoned across the nothingness I focused on behind my closed eyelids. They said:

I'm obviously unlovable. I'm a loser. Of course every man is going to dump me. I'm fucked up. I'm a mess. I'm a failure. I'm nobody.

I'm nobody. I'm nobody.

*

(I once met Sting in a restaurant and gushed about how much I liked the production of one of his albums that a friend of a friend of mine had played on. He thanked me and asked, "And who are you?"

"I'm Nobody," I said.)

I would be on my own forever, my thoughts announced, because I was unfit for a relationship. *Obviously* no one was ever going to date me again. Who, in their right mind, would date me?

"I will," said the voice.

What?

Even though it sounded like the voice came from someone sitting right in front of me, almost nose-to-nose with me, I didn't open my eyes. Partly because I obviously knew there would be no one there and partly because I didn't know what I'd do if there was!

Suddenly I became aware that I couldn't hear the general muffled sounds of the beach life around me. It was as if someone had put ear mufflers on me. For a moment I half wondered if I'd fallen asleep sitting upright and was dreaming. But I could *feel* things, like the heat of the sun, and the wind, and the sand under me.

Who would ever date me? I asked again, in my head, slowly. The response was immediate.

"I will."

I hadn't imagined it. (Or I had, but had skilfully imagined it again.)

Now, in my mind's eye, I saw a white shape in the distance. I focused on it and it started to grow bigger; it was moving towards me. Eventually I could make it out as the shape of a body. A figure was coming towards me. It was all white. And it *kept* coming towards me, slowly. Then I could see that the figure was a woman, and I started to make out her face and… she was *me*! She was a much more beautiful *version* of me, she had the clearest skin and the brightest eyes, and a serene expression on her face, but it was recognizably *my* face.

The imaginary me got closer and closer until it actually went right into me. And suddenly I felt completely different. I felt calm and strong. I had the sense that I needed to look after this imaginary being, that she was worth protecting, that it was my *job* to protect her.

A moment later, the sounds of the beach returned, as if someone had restored the volume after hitting the mute button. I could hear children laughing and shouting in the distance. I opened my eyes and discovered that the world was still there. Everything was how it was before.

Except that it wasn't.

Something had definitely changed. I just wasn't sure what yet. But on the long walk back to the car, I was preoccupied with one thing. If I was the one who'd said, "I will" to the question, "Who would date me?" what did that imply? That I should date myself? What a ridiculous idea.

Or was it?

If *I* was the common denominator, in every relationship that went wrong, if it wasn't them, if it was definitely *me* that was the issue here, then could this be a way of getting to the bottom of the problem?

Could I date myself and see what was up? What made me such a disaster, someone no one wanted? Well *that* didn't sound like much fun. But there was something in it. Maybe I could make it fun.

Okay, I decided. I'll do it! I will swear off men for a whole year. No matter what happens, I told myself, *no dating*. That was the rule. I could only date *me*. And I had to actually, physically do it; I had to take myself out *on dates*.

If nothing else, I'd have a good time. (What else was I going to do with my life?)

Now... where should I take me first?

"Well, now that we have seen each other," said the Unicorn, "If you'll believe in me, I'll believe in you. Is that a bargain?"

Through the Looking Glass,
Chapter 7

LEWIS CARROLL

CHAPTER THREE

The Girl Who Dated Herself

My first date was a speed date.

It was kind of perfect timing that the lease on my apartment in Los Feliz was coming to an end. It was a cheap, soulless joint that I'd taken because it was an affordable large one bedroom and I needed space for the boyfriend to come visit from England. Which he did once before announcing that he wouldn't come again until the TV show was commissioned and I had a six-figure salary coming in, so that I could pay for our lifestyle.

Seemed fair to me.

Still believing, somewhat naïvely, that the green light would come through any day and I'd soon have enough money for the dream beach house, I didn't want to commit to anything within my tiny budget for too long. A friend of a friend knew an actress who needed to sublet her place in Silver Lake for a couple of months while she went on location to shoot a movie. It sounded ideal.

I had made a plan to see it that very evening, so I headed there on my way back from the beach (taking the 10 to the 110 to the 101 but getting off at Benton instead of Vermont).

★

Set on one of the highest points in the Silver Lake hills, a short (albeit steep) walk up from the Sunset Triangle, was a stunning two-storey 1930s Spanish style house nestling within a veritable jungle of indigenous succulents and tall imported palms, on a steep plot of land. At the foot of this oasis was a stand-alone two-car garage and atop this structure, the owner had built a studio apartment, part of which was built *around* the chunky trunk of a Jacaranda tree that grew beside the garage, providing a striking purple canopy in the current flowering season.

The apartment was known to all its occupants as… *The Treehouse*.

Two weeks later, I was its latest occupant.

The packing, the moving and a new round of notes from the producers kept me occupied for those two weeks. The nicotine cravings hadn't completely stopped, but I was in control now. I'd had stern words with My Nicotine Addiction after that dramatic meltdown. I explained that there would be no more nicotine… ever! There would not be "just one" on a special occasion. There would not be any patches or gum or e-cigs. I calmly explained that I could never, ever risk going through the pain and drama of that night again. He would rear his ugly head every now and again but I would politely remind him who was in charge and he would pipe down again.

This was also timely, given that I was about to date myself; I had always preferred to date non-smokers.

The change of environment also helped with the cravings. I could never dream of soiling somewhere so beautiful with nasty smoke.

Living in the treehouse reminded me of a childhood book I'd loved: Enid Blyton's *The Magic Faraway Tree*. The story featured an enormous, enchanted tree in which various creatures resided. I would often come home to my little piece of paradise expecting to run into Moon-Face, Silky the Fairy, or The Saucepan Man. It was heart-warming.

There was a tiny, private terrace in the corner of the front yard of the main house that was only accessible from the steps that led up to the treehouse. It had a fire pit, two Adirondack chairs and the most spectacular, panoramic view stretching from the protruding sky-scrapers of Downtown across the whole of the L.A. basin. You could see the KTLA radio tower and the W Hotel in Hollywood, the office buildings of Century City beyond, another cluster of high-rises along the Wilshire corridor in Westwood, and on a clear day you could even see a slither of silver demarcating the Pacific Ocean, shimmering on the horizon.

Sundown was a particularly magical time. As the sun sank in the west, it reflected off the vast expanse of glass on those Downtown monoliths, making them look like shiny gold nuggets sticking out of the eastern horizon.

Inside the treehouse, the current tenant had decked the place out beautifully, with funky furniture, and plenty of gadgets and chachkies from Bed, Bath & Beyond. I loved living someone else's life.

Anyone else's would have felt better than mine at that point.

Bookcases separated the kitchen and the main room, which had large built-in closets. The bathroom was also "built-in"… built in to one of the closets. You opened the sliding closet doors and there was a toilet on one side and a tiny bathtub with a shower over it on the other: a true W.C. (water closet). There was no room for a hand basin; hands were washed and teeth were brushed at the kitchen sink. The massive king-sized bed took pride of place in the centre of the room under a skylight. On my first night it rained (a rare occurrence in Los Angeles) and I fell asleep to the soothing sound of raindrops above me, the tree's canopy breaking their fall so they didn't hit the glass too hard.

I'd never lived anywhere so charming and peaceful.

This was a good place to start my new journey. I could feel it.

For the first couple of weeks, while we went through an unseasonal cold snap, I holed up in the treehouse, cocooned away from the real world. I broke a lifetime's rule and worked in bed, propping myself up against the colourful collection of oversized pillows my sub-landlady had art-fully assembled.

As well as working on the notes on the pilot (that was rapidly losing any resemblance to the show I'd originally envisioned), I'd had an idea for a screenplay that was set in nineteenth-century New York, so I busied myself with research for that.

I spent my writing breaks sipping coffee on the tranquil terrace or curled up in the den (a corner of the main room that was sectioned off with a huge couch) watching re-runs of *Everybody Loves Raymond* and *Friends*. On Saturdays, I shopped at the Silver Lake Farmers' Market. I lived off vegetable tamales that I bought by the dozen and kept in the freezer, and Korean food from Dave's stall.

Several blissful days flew by before I tapped myself on

the shoulder and said, "Um, hello, how about that first date you promised me?"

There was a French bistro on Vermont that I had regularly walked past, dreaming (as I stole furtive glances at diners on dates) of the night when some new, fabulous boyfriend would take me there.

So, to hell with him, *I* would take me there.

The second I walked through the door, I knew I had made a terrible mistake. The corner diner up the street, with an eat-at counter perfect for single diners would have been the smarter choice. This place, of course, was full of couples; it was designed for them, with tiny tables for two, where their knees could touch and they could converse in romantic whispers. I looked around. All couples. There was one party of six (but obviously made up of three couples) sitting at a group of tables that had been pushed together near the window, and a table of four (a couple with two adorable young children, one a sleeping baby in a stroller), but apart from that… the place was filled with loved-up couples.

This was definitely the wrong place for me but now the Maître d' was approaching and the embarrassment of saying I needed a table for one compared with the embarrassment of saying I'd changed my mind was the lesser of two evils.

"Table for two?" he asked, grabbing two menus from a stand near the door.

"Um, no, it's just me," I murmured, apologetically. He gave me a pitying smile and replaced one of the menus.

"This way please," he said, indicating I should follow him to the back of the restaurant.

"Actually, is that table there free?" I asked, pointing to a tiny table in the window, beside the party of six. The Maître d' stared at me.

"You want to sit up front with everyone staring at you as they walk in, thinking what's wrong with you that you need to eat alone in a nice restaurant on a Saturday night, feeling sorry for you, wondering why you're such a loser?" he asked. No, of course he didn't… but his expression did, as he seated me at the table I'd indicated.

I opened the little paper packet in my water glass and started chewing on a grissini. What was I thinking? Why had I chosen this place? And why had I chosen a Saturday night, traditional date night? Why not take myself out on a Tuesday? It's not like I had to fit around my date's schedule.

I had not thought this through.

Earlier that evening I had felt so smug about the fact that I didn't need to make any kind of effort if I was just dating myself. It was a relief not to worry about what I was going to wear, whether my hair was going to behave, which shade of lipstick would look least or most (depending on what I was going for) slutty. I didn't have to fret over shoes I could barely walk in. I could wear my glasses instead of using a pair of daily contact lenses from my rapidly diminishing stock. I certainly didn't have to shave my legs. But now, amongst all these trendy East-siders (even the baby was in a Bugaboo stroller) I felt painfully self-conscious in my unfashionable boot-cut jeans, faded H&M t-shirt and unwashed hair. I had half a mind to bolt for the door, but as he'd handed me the menu, the Maître d' had given me a look to suggest that I should think myself extremely fortunate to be allowed to sit up front with the normal people, so I didn't dare move.

So what does one do on a dinner date with oneself? That's a really good question and another one I hadn't thought to ask myself before I was sitting, staring at the baby, wondering how to entertain myself. There's a scene in an episode of *Sex and the City* where Carrie goes to a restaurant by herself, without a date, without a book, and just sits there, enjoying her own company. In TV time the scene takes about twelve seconds. I could manage twelve seconds; anyone could manage *twelve seconds*.

How does one get through an hour?

The baby was waking up so, once I'd ordered my glass of Sancerre and *frites* with a side of *frites* (not much else for a non-meat eater in a French bistro), I occupied myself with entertaining him instead.

But it's not normal to be able to play peek-a-boo for a solid thirty minutes, as the baby's father indicated by drawing the stroller a little closer to his table, protectively, after throwing a wary look in my direction. So I amused myself by eavesdropping on the table of six, who were not speaking in romantic whispers.

"We can't take our nanny to Hawaii, she's illegal, so we're taking Seth's niece. She's a freshman at Berkley. Seth's brother won't let her do Spring Break so—"

"—if he wants my Knicks tickets that weekend, we could switch for a Lakers game in the New Year—"

"—only one point five, and then they tried to screw me on the back end."

The usual L.A. soundtrack.

I was soon bored. At least on a bad date I could use the

guy as a sounding board while I basically talked about myself… *to* myself. I didn't think talking to myself without the façade of a listener was a good idea at this point. I was already getting increasingly suspicious glances from both the Maître d' and the Bugaboo Daddy, so I downed my wine and shovelled the last of my fries into my mouth, then I paid the check and vacated the table for one of the two couples waiting in the entrance foyer… and also looking at me with undisguised disdain.

I was home and in bed by 9.30pm.

My first date was a speed date.

The pilot rewrite and the screenplay research aside, I wasn't terribly busy. Apparently no one needed me. The phone was silent. It had been so long since I'd had an email from anyone, I sent one to myself to check my account was still working.

I got into a good routine of taking a morning walk every day, through the hills, around the reservoir, and back. On some days, saying "good morning" to the three or four dog walkers I passed on my route was the only time I spoke to or saw another human being that day. Even they, I felt, looked at me strangely, as if wondering why I walked alone. Where was my dog? Man, I was such a loser… I didn't even have a dog.

So I was tentatively excited when I got an invitation to a party. One of Greg's client/friends, an entertainment lawyer called Monty who lived with his South African boyfriend (a one-time Olympic swimmer, now personal trainer) in an architectural award-winning home made of metal and glass in the Hollywood Hills was throwing a "small and intimate holiday party" for around 300 guests.

The invitation was for me "plus one".

I graciously accepted my kind offer to join myself.

The Hollywood Hills, if you are not familiar, is an area that is anathema to even the most mildly claustrophobic person. The foothills are a labyrinth of winding streets, filled with parked cars, dense with badly constructed houses that have all partially slid on top of each other during earthquakes and landslides, and are now barely separated by makeshift pieces of timber and steel. The air is thick with the aroma of overgrown jasmine plants and other lush vegetation (that no one has had the time or energy to prune since having to cancel the gardening service when their TV show – the one that bought them the house in the first place – got cancelled.)

But there is some light (and air) once you get to the top, and the views are worth the effort.

As I navigated the Saturn around the hairpin bends that led up to the top of Lookout Mountain Avenue, I rehearsed my speech for the unavoidable valet. (The only way to ensure people actually come to your party, if you live in the Hollywood Hills, is to write COMPLIMENTARY VALET PARKING at the top of the invitation; it's way more important than even the date or time.)

"Listen," I began as I stepped out of my car, looking up into the face of a well-groomed kid with a ripped body who was convinced he would be "spotted" by a director whose car he got to park and get cast in the next big summer blockbuster. When I'd driven nicer cars I often reclaimed my vehicle back from the valet to find a headshot and resume left on the passenger seat. But I was clearly a Nobody so this guy was already looking over the top of my head.

"Excuse me," I said, a little louder. He looked at me, blankly. "This is really, *really* important. You mustn't put my car into Park, okay?"

"No problem, ma'am," he auto-replied back at me in a monotone. I knew he wasn't paying attention so I tried to lock eyes with him.

"No, I'm serious. You *have* to leave it in Neutral and then use the parking brake. If you put it in Park, it'll probably get stuck. Please *promise* me you'll leave it in Neutral when you park it up. I've maxed out my Triple A call-outs for the year. They will charge me for any more."

He was looking at me but he was million miles away. Probably practicing his Oscar acceptance speech.

"Only. In. Neutral. Okay?" I demanded, loudly.

"No problem, ma'am." I wondered if he *was* an android. I wouldn't put it past Monty to be trying the latest AI gadgets. But, no, a computer program would have given me more attention.

I gave up. I looked at the time: 8pm. Saturday night. Holiday season. I weighed the odds. If I put in the call now I might be out of there by midnight. It was worth the $60. I brought up Triple A's number on my phone; it was on speed dial.

The guest list was Hollywood D-list, a few "reality show" celebrities, lawyers and accountants with mildly impressive client lists, and the GRS boys. That's the Gay Rocket Scientists – the name Greg and I had given to an ex of his who worked at JPL (NASA's research facility at Caltech) and his gang, who were always invited to these parties to provide a certain wow factor. They weren't all easy on the eye but, boy, could they wipe the floor with anyone in a conversation about anything even remotely important! They could also be relied upon not to know anyone famous on account of them not watching TV or following anything in the media. And celebs (especially the lesser known ones) *love* to be incognito. The protocol at these parties was that you *never* mentioned where you knew someone from if you recognized them. It didn't matter how famous they were. You could find yourself standing next to Heather Locklear at the buffet table and much as you might be dying to ask her what it was really like *Livin' On A Prayer* you mustn't ask anything more significant than, "Have you tried the shrimp? They're delicious."

It was fine, however, if *they* brought up their career.

Thus I got trapped under the huge spiral staircase talking to an actor I vaguely recognized from *NCIS* or *Bones* or *Criminal Minds* (I was a light drama/comedy girl; the cop shows all blended into one for me) about how many pilots he'd tested for before he got his big break.

My eyes were frantically searching for a waitress carrying a tray of the delicious chocolate nutmeg martinis that were being served, when I saw *him*.

My Crush of the Century was there. Of course he was.

Gavin James was an investment banker. Investment bankers didn't generally circulate in Hollywood, their natural habitat being Wall Street, Connecticut at the weekends, and Martha's Vineyard in the summer (the west coast was considered kind of tacky), but Gavin James had been dabbling in film financing. He and Monty were planning to launch a niche distribution company.

I'd met Gavin at a birthday dinner Monty had thrown for Greg at the Chateau Marmont earlier that year. In fact just a week before the boyfriend had dumped me, out of the blue, and my world had fallen apart.

Gavin and I had been seated opposite each other at the dinner. We'd talked about England a lot. He'd done his MBA in London after getting his degree in Philosophy, Politics and Economics from Oxford University. He'd been at Christ Church to be exact, the college that had rejected me after a gruelling interview when I was 17. He was dreamy in ways I had never dreamed of. He had recently split up with his fiancée because she wanted to move back to France and he didn't want to settle there. Although he enjoyed their summers with her family in the Dordogne region, he could never contemplate setting up home and *"raising kids there"* I vividly remember him saying. I had felt a twinge of something. I wasn't single then, of course, but it wouldn't have mattered if I had been; he was so far out of my league I wouldn't have even qualified for a day pass to *visit* his league. But I still fantasised about him, about us being together in a parallel universe in which I *had* got into Christ Church at the same time as him and we'd become everyone's favourite couple.

He was my Mr Big.

I had thought about him intensely, for a whole week. But then the break-up had thrown me such a curve ball I had literally not given him a second thought… until I saw him that night.

"ExcusemeIjustsawsomeoneIhavetosayhelloto," I virtually spat at the *NCIS* actor as I propelled myself with the force of one of the GRS boys' rocket launchers towards my future.

I had to follow Gavin through a tightly packed crowd (the architectural award-winning house's capacity had definitely been breached), out onto the deck. I cut him off by going around the narrower end of the triangular swimming pool and kind of collided with him by the hot tub, hastily trying to make it look like I'd ended up there by wandering, randomly, into the vicinity.

"Hey! You're back," I gushed, slightly out of breath from my obstacle course race. "How was China?" I just remembered he'd been off on a three-month long business trip to China when we'd met... banker stuff.

"It was good, thank you!"

My mouth went so dry, my tongue stuck to the roof of my mouth. *Where* were those waitresses with the martinis? He filled the silence. "So how are *you*? What's new?"

Well after my boyfriend of five years dumped me, I cried myself to sleep for two months straight. I got rejected by a guy I picked up in a bar who had a pencil for a penis, then by a man who I think might have been sleeping with both his dog and his mother. I had a mini nervous breakdown when I discovered I was a total nicotine addict and then decided that I wouldn't date any more men, I'd just date myself, but that is obviously a STUPID idea so I am completely free to date you and marry you (next Thursday if you're free) and raise all our beautiful children several thousands of miles away from the Dordogne region.

"Oh, nothing much," I managed, finding some emergency saliva from somewhere. I smiled, nodding my head profusely, nervously, and added, "You look well." He laughed. Oh that sexy laugh. I forgot he had *such* a sexy laugh; like a good Syrah, from the better part of France, full of silky bass notes.

"I don't think so!" He patted his (clearly rock solid) belly. "Everything I ate in China was cooked in pork fat. I don't know how their arteries cope. I've been off the carbs for six months straight, ever since I got back, and I still feel sluggish."

Finally, a waitress wandered between us with a tray of cocktails. I grabbed two. Gavin, who I suddenly noticed was holding a bottle of Perrier, politely declined. "Driving," he muttered, half to me, half to the waitress. I looked down at my drinks, suddenly embarrassed. He looked at them, too, then asked (making an obvious deduction), "Is your boyfriend here?"

I took a very large swig of the martini in my right hand.

"No, we broke up." And my heart skipped a beat because I *definitely* saw a flicker of something in his eye… a fractional raise of an eyebrow… the hint of a smile. I drained the rest of the martini in my right hand before adding, before he'd even said anything, "It's okay. It was time. We'd run our course."

What on earth should I say or do next?

With impeccable – bordering on comical – timing, a stunning, petite, Chinese girl of, I'd guess, around twenty-two, maybe twenty-three, appeared and slipped into the compact space between the left side of Gavin's body and his muscular, outstretched arm, a space I couldn't have fitted into if I'd stopped eating for two years. She smiled, pleasantly, at me. He beamed at her and then looked back at me.

"This is Su-Lin." And this time I clearly saw the eyebrow go up a little, there was no mistaking that slightly awkward smile and I knew exactly what was going on. He wasn't interested in me; he'd completely forgotten my name.

"Hi…" I squealed. "I'm Jessica. I've heard lovely things about you." I had no idea what compelled me to lie. "I have to take this—" Damn, he already knew I had no one to take the martini in my left hand to. "—to the loo. I mean, I have to *go*... to the loo." I was dying a quick but painful death. "Could you hold this for me, actually?" And I shoved the spare drink into Su-Lin's hand before she had time to answer. "Berightback," I hissed at her.

I went in search of Monty. I never feel right leaving a party without thanking the hostess. It's just not polite. In my first incarnation in Los Angeles, I'd caught a so-called friend lying, saying he'd been at a party I'd given but hadn't seen me. But I knew he'd been at a party he considered to be more important than mine, because I knew the girl he had taken as his date and she'd been decent enough to come clean to me about needing to go to the more important party.

Whenever people said, "Great party," or "Loved your movie," in L.A. you could almost guarantee they hadn't attended or seen it.

As I got close, Monty grabbed me and cuddled me until his underarm sweat transferred damp patches onto the sleeves of my blouse. He was a gay man but had a peculiar penchant for fondling girls in a way that, had he been heterosexual, would have led to lawsuits. We let him because there was truly nothing sexual in it. He was just desperate for affection. He and the South African clearly had something going on because they'd been together for years, but his boyfriend barely acknowledged him in public, let alone touched him.

"Jessica, sweetheart! Don't be a stranger! You've had a rough year! Where are you for the holidays? You must come to us! Don't be on your own!" Monty always communicated by shouting everything in short sentences. He was even louder when he was drunk.

I told Monty I was planning to go back to the U.K. to spend it with family. At that point, even though I still hadn't bought my ticket and was dreading my first visit back and facing the weirdness of navigating my London life without the boyfriend, it was the truth.

While I stood in line to get my car from the valet – with all my fingers crossed that he'd heeded my instructions, I noticed a silver Porsche Boxster parked beside the valet stand. I knew the type who drove those, probably one of Monty's lawyer pals, one of the ones who had slightly different intentions than Monty when fondling the girls. I wondered how much the ugly, fat, sweaty womanizer had tipped the valet to keep it in this prime spot.

I turned to look down the hill and my heart sank as I saw the valet guy I'd given my ticket to walking back to the stand with my keys, minus my car. He looked puzzled as he approached me.

"Ma'am, your car's like stuck in Park."

While I waited for Triple A, praising myself for putting in that call at 8pm, I set up camp on the steps beside the jasmine plants and sulked. I channelled my funk at the Boxster. It suddenly represented all that was wrong with the world; all that was wrong with men. I glared at it; wishing some grave misfortune would befall the owner, like his dick would fall off, or he'd get the most painful haemorrhoids.

With a stroke of luck I hardly deserved given my evil cursing of all Porsche owners, I happened to glance at the front door just as Gavin and his Chinese souvenir emerged from the house, giving me time to get to my feet and back into the bushes so they wouldn't see me. I sank deeper and deeper into their wispy fronds as I watched *my* future husband (in another life) pop his doll into the passenger seat, climb in and drive off.

The beautiful smell of jasmine was forever ruined for me.

Two hours later (Triple A were super apologetic but it *was* the holidays) I scolded myself severely as I found myself unconsciously singing Bowie's 'China Girl' on my winding drive back down to Sunset.

> *My little China girl*
> *You shouldn't mess with me*
> *I'll ruin everything you are...*

"At any rate I'll never go THERE again!" said Alice as she picked her way through the wood. "It's the stupidest tea-party I ever was at in all my life!"

Alice's Adventures in Wonderland,
Chapter 7

LEWIS CARROLL

CHAPTER FOUR

The Girl Who Cancelled Christmas

I'm a mug, what are you?

The next day, I officially cancelled Christmas.

I don't think the family were all that surprised. I'd barely communicated with them that year. There was a distinct lack of sympathy for me in the aftermath of the break-up. Very little "Are you okay?" and lots of, "You brought this on yourself, Jessica. You can't expect a man to wait forever for you. If you focus on your career and neglect your relationship, what do you expect?" An undertone of misogyny ran through the blood on both sides of the family, even the female blood. Strong women, who claimed to be feminists, usually bowed down to the patriarchy when challenged. I had always tried my best to stand up to this, but along with my "very precarious way to earn a living" (being a writer) and my "idealistic and delusional left-wing views", I wasn't so much the "black sheep" (a title officially taken by my cousin who'd dropped out of Cambridge to marry a beautiful Venezuelan girl and now ran a barely solvent yoga teacher training business in Costa Rica), I was simply a sheep of some dubious colour that no one could quite describe.

I also didn't tell any of my L.A. friends that I *wasn't* going home. I suddenly felt obliged to spend Christmas on my own. Could I really do that? After two somewhat lacklustre dates, I was a little dubious. But I needed to try. Every Christmas I could remember had been a big old production, with all the cooking and the shopping and the negotiating between various factions of the family – everyone wanting things organized a slightly different way. What kind of Christmas could I give myself if I channelled all my efforts into giving myself what *I* wanted instead of worrying about everyone else's needs?

On Christmas Eve I found myself traipsing up and down the packed aisles of the Pasadena Whole Foods (commonly known amongst my friends as "Whole Pay Check" on account of the fact that it was impossible to enter and leave the store spending anything less than $100) on South Arroyo Parkway salivating. I'd forgotten the cardinal rule: never shop on an empty stomach, and the pile in my cart was steadily growing. I was beginning to look like I was making a feast for fifteen, as opposed to a couple of meals for one!

As I watched happy couples and mothers carrying their babies in slings fill *their* shopping carts with holiday fare – organic apple pies, chocolate Santas, sugar cookies, candied walnuts, peppermint bark, caramel popcorn, plastic tubs of assorted mezze from the deli counter, whole sides of salmon from the fish counter, chestnuts, cranberries and sacks of tangerines, something painful began gnawing at my insides.

I was going through the motions. I was trying to be nice to myself. I was outwardly saying, "I *deserve* this. I *will* take care of myself," and inwardly saying, *"Loser!"* The big pile of food in my cart screamed at me, "There's no one but you to eat all this, you pathetic, greedy pig!"

Realizing that Whole Foods was not the place for me, I abandoned my cart in the middle of the wine section and headed for the place that made it easier for Losers to lose themselves: Target. There was nowhere else like it in the world. In the U.K. we had John Lewis (too fancy) and Woolworths (too tacky) but nowhere so perfectly pitched at people who just wanted some nice-looking things that didn't cost the earth.

Specifically, I chose TarGay. Greg and his friends had renamed and claimed this particular Target as it was in West Hollywood. They had gone on to name many others, for example "Targenega" on South La Cienega, "Tar-get-away" in Culver City (because of its proximity to the airport) and "Target-about-it" in North Hollywood because it was so far away it wasn't worth going to.

There was a rumour that the nicknames had reached staff in the stores and management weren't too happy about it, which delighted Greg and co.

The patrons of TarGay were a particularly eclectic crowd. Hollywood managers mingled with Mexican nannies; high-strung real estate agents fought over the last multipacks of Doublemint and Juicy Fruit gum with high school kids.

You could never blend in but you would never stand out. I could make it my very own Loserville.

I usually relished Christmas shopping. It was the only time of the year I *did* enjoy shopping. At all other times, the very thought of shopping triggered an anxiety rash. But venturing out for a few hours to buy gifts for other people always filled me with joy. I loved buying gifts, I loved wrapping them, I loved writing the little gift tags, I loved tying ribbons around the packages and, most of all, I loved giving them.

The ex and I had kept up a tradition of giving each other Christmas stockings. Every year, we would fill each other's stocking with cheap, frivolous gifts… some fun, some useful, but everything (on my side, anyway) well chosen.

As I fingered the red felt stocking with the yellow and brown reindeer shapes stuck around the cuff, I fought back the tears. I loved this aisle the most; it was the one with all the gift bags and gift wrap and ribbons and gift tags and (at this time of year) stockings and Santa sacks.

I took a deep breath. Okay, I could do this. On one level, it felt ridiculous, but I had to do it. I put the stocking in my basket along with a roll of red and gold gift wrap and a bundle of gold ribbon.

I powered through the aisles of TarGay picking up an assortment of pretty crap I didn't need. A post-it-note holder, some turquoise "salt spray" bath salts, a yellow jasmine (forgetting my newly acquired aversion) scented candle, a pair of elf-on-the-shelf socks, a logo (the Rolling Stones one with the mouth and tongue sticking out) T-shirt (XXL, so I could hide inside), a pack of Red Vines (still my preferred nicotine substitute), a bag of Jelly Belly sours. Would I really date someone who bought me this crap? I doubted whether even the ex – not known for his prowess in choosing gifts – had ever assembled such a sorry selection of goods.

By the checkout, I noticed a mug that said, "I'm a mug, what are you?" That the British interpretation of this would probably be lost on most Americans made me smile. Even though the truth of it stung.

A "mug" in British slang is someone who is a bit of a fool, someone who will do a lot for other people for nothing in return, or someone who can be conned, have their chain yanked, be made fun of easily.

At last I had found the perfect gift for me.

I did feel like a right mug. I'd convinced myself that I was someone who could become a successful screenwriter, but the producers were giving me the total run around and I was letting them. I had persuaded myself that my rugby-loving, beer-swilling, emotionally repressed boyfriend was the one for me, and had stuck by him while he made very little effort with me, for five years. I'd totally bought into the idea that I could achieve what I saw other people achieving, that I knew where I was heading and had a route planned out to get there.

I'd totally conned myself. It was all one big farce. The reality was, I knew nothing, not even what I really wanted out of life.

Except mango sorbet.

I knew I wanted mango sorbet. So I stopped off at Trader Joe's on the way home and picked up some cheap wine, several bags of frozen nasi goreng, popping corn, some chocolate-coated almonds and two tubs of mango sorbet.

If Christmas was cancelled, to hell with tradition, I could eat what I liked.

On Christmas morning I woke with a start at 6am. It was still dark out. My head hurt. Damn the cheap Trader Joe's wine! Every time!

I'd enjoyed the previous night's festivities for one. I'd found some of my favourite classic movies amongst my sub-landlady's collection: *Some Like It Hot*, *All About Eve*, and *North by Northwest*. I'd spent the evening watching movies, munching popcorn and wrapping my little gifts. Everything got gift wrapped, including the Jelly Bellys and Red Vines; everything except the mug… because I'd drunk the wine out of it. I'd added a sachet of mulling spices to the wine and a little apple juice and then microwaved it to make it into a rather tasty mulled wine, which is what convinced me to drink so much of it. The old "most of the alcohol burns off" excuse had been rolled out every year by the alcoholic contingent of my family and I was still a sucker for it.

I lay in bed staring up through the skylight at the patches of sky I could see through the tree branches. I watched as it slowly changed from black to dark purple. I could just make out a star. I was completely alone on Christmas morning. I had never woken up alone in a house on Christmas morning before; I'd always been in a family member's home, or with a boyfriend, or with friends.

I assumed I should feel sad but, apart from my aching head, I actually felt okay. What was the big deal? Christmas had never held any religious significance in my family. It was mostly a time when there would be a lot of drama. People would get drunk and drag up unresolved past griev-ances. There would be a scramble to get the food ready with a massively unfair division of labour (the boys doing nothing and the girls doing everything) that would turn into simmering resentment, which would eventually grow into big clouds of anger that rained down passive-aggressive jibes. There would be too much food, *far* too much food. My mother would grumble for an hour after it was confirmed that my sister was *"still* a vegetarian"*, swearing she'd seen her eat chicken two weeks ago. Someone would cheat at Monopoly but the wrong person would get accused and storm off. There would be too much wine drunk, always *far* too much wine drunk. And when we were all forced outside for a "nice walk" everyone would claim they thought someone else had been responsible for closing the door when we got back and found it wide open and the cat long gone.

So rather than feel lonely and sad, a sense of peace washed over me that morning and I felt almost proud of myself for facing my first Christmas completely alone. I appreciated the sense of relief that I had no obligations, that I could choose exactly how I wanted to spend my day.

I looked over to the couch where I saw a gift-filled stocking.

"Santa's been!" I thought for a split second before I remembered the truth. And I was about to leap out of bed and start tearing them open when I realized I didn't have to do it right then and there. There was no one shouting at me from downstairs, warning me that we were "OPENING PRESENTS IN FIVE MINUTES!"

I went for an extra long morning walk. When I got back I had a quick shower and then got back into my pyjamas (because there was no one to tell me not to) before opening my presents. I ate chocolate-covered almonds for breakfast and then the whole bag of Jelly Bellys as I lay on the couch watching *Sex and the City* from the start. I took a long nap at 4pm. By the evening, as I sat down on the couch to eat my Christmas dinner of microwaved nasi goreng followed by mango sorbet, I was halfway through season two. It was a highly successful Christmas dinner; no one made me wear a stupid paper crown, there were no bad, sexist jokes, and no one spilled red wine on the carpet causing a half-hour hiatus in proceedings while it got cleaned up.

All Christmas Days should be like this, I decided.

The week between Christmas and New Year I spent pretty much doing more of the same. I got into a kind of routine. I walked, I watched movies and re-runs of my favourite TV shows, I ate, I wrote a little… but nothing to write home about. I got into taking these long naps. I'd never been a daytime napper (and was jealous of people who were), so I considered it something of an achievement.

I was so proud of myself for nailing the "Solo Christmas" concept I assumed "Solo New Year's Eve" would be a breeze. I'll make it into a proper date, I thought.

Remembering how despondent I'd felt sitting in the French bistro, looking like I'd just crawled out of bed, I resolved to make a little more effort on this date. I dug out a never-worn H&M dress and dusted off some high-heeled sandals.

I washed my hair and as I was drying it my eyes fell on the little bag of make-up in my basket of toiletries. I'd never been a big make-up wearer, I certainly didn't put it on as a rule every day, but I wouldn't have dreamed of going on a real date without at least a little powder, mascara and lipstick. But to put on make-up when I was just going to be out with me? It felt faintly ridiculous so I dismissed the idea.

I was ready at 6pm. That felt as good a time as ever to

leave the house to go for dinner (I thought, forgetting it was New Year's Eve.)

I'd been eying up a little restaurant in the area with some curiosity. It was on the corner of Sunset and Maltman but you couldn't see anything that was going on behind the tall bamboo fence around it. Judging by the valet lines, though, it was popular.

Deciding this was the perfect occasion to try out the mysterious establishment, I shuffled down the hill in my heels (another factor I hadn't really thought through… these were car to bar stool heels, I had no business trying to walk four blocks in them, most of it on a 30-degrees incline). I thought to myself, if the restaurant felt too fancy, was too expensive or fully booked, I'd try my luck at Café Stella.

Wise to *all* the rookie mistakes I'd made on my first date, I took a book.

To watch me totter down that hill in those heels, you'd have thought I was already staggering home drunk after a huge night out. What should have been a five-minute walk took me around twenty to complete. I arrived at the restaurant just before half past six. The valet guys were not even out yet. Suddenly I worried that it might be closed. But I pushed on the bamboo gate and it opened.

What lay beyond the bamboo perimeter was utterly charming. There was a large courtyard with fairy lights hanging low over wooden tables that were clustered around water features and stone sculptures and fire pits. There wasn't a soul in sight. Nor was there any silverware on the tables. I immediately felt rather stupid for coming out so early. Maybe this was the point of a relationship… to have someone to stop you from doing *really* stupid things.

I walked into the bar area where there were a few more tables… but still no people. So I perched on a stool at the bar and took out my book. I was in no hurry. I was re-reading Eckhart Tolle's *A New Earth*, hoping it would help me figure out what part of my subconscious might still be unconscious and what I could do to revive it. Perhaps *it* could stop me from doing really stupid things.

As I busied myself with living in "the now", a kitchen porter walked through the bar carrying some boxes. I tried to smile at him as he walked past but he looked straight ahead, as if I was invisible. Perhaps I wasn't working hard enough to be in "the now"; maybe I wasn't even really there. I focused on the book with a little more intensity until a loud crunching sound made me jump. I looked up to see a girl behind the bar pouring ice cubes into a what looked like a giant blender that was spitting out the crushed ice into a bucket below.

The girl was tall and stick thin. She had no boobs to speak of. She was dressed all in black: black t-shirt, black jeans, black army boots. She even had cropped black hair and was wearing lots of black eye make-up. The only colour, any-where on this woman's body was the bright red lipstick on her mouth. The whole effect was incredibly sexy and one that I knew, sadly, I could never pull off. She looked incredibly young. I doubted she was more than 17. I considered asking her for *her* ID.

"Hi," I said, over the noise of the blender. Surely she had seen me sitting there. She didn't seem to hear me.

"Hi!" I shouted. She looked up at me briefly and then looked down and carried on crushing the ice. I watched her. I was less important than ice. Okay.

Finally she finished, switched off the blender and started

pouring the ice into a metal tub filled with champagne bottles.

"Are you actually open?" I asked finally, assuming she'd say no and tell me what time they *did* open.

"Yeah."

"Can I order a drink?" Or a needle to stab myself in the eye with, which would be marginally less painful that this conversation.

She put her hands on her hips and sighed.

"Sure. Whatdoyouwant?"

I desperately wanted to say, "You know what, it feels like it's too much trouble for you, which is fine, but I'd rather be in a place that makes me feel more comfortable so I think I'll just leave," or rather have my date say that before sweeping me out of there. But I'd never learned to stand up to bullies. In fact the meaner they were, the more I tried to ingratiate myself. So I just said, "Surprise me."

Ice girl rolled her eyes, reached below the bar and retrieved a smaller blender, which she placed on the bar, and then started crushing more ice.

Two minutes later she put a strawberry daiquiri in front of me.

I hate strawberry daiquiris.

Ice girl turned her attention to cutting up a bowl full of limes into segments.

"I'm on a hot date tonight," I informed her, for no good reason, and with no regard for my dignity whatsoever.

"Cool," she replied, robotically. You could argue that there was no reason for her to have any interest in my life. And *again*, you see here the perfect opportunity for me to throw ten bucks down on the counter and get up and leave. Not me. I said, "You probably think he's meeting me later."

She said nothing but glanced at me, her eyes saying, *STOP TALKING TO ME NOW!*

"But he's not," I enthused for no reason other than to set the scene for the upcoming moment of complete and utter humiliation. "Because I'm actually on a date with myself."

Her eyes now asked, *why? Why are you doing this to yourself? Be pathetic if you must, but don't advertise it to the world.* Or perhaps that was just me projecting.

I sucked some juice out of my daiquiri, which was 99% ice.

"How much for the drink?"

"Eleven dollars."

I put the cash on the bar and fled.

I contemplated Café Stella but I was feeling so deflated I just got some tacos from the taco stand and walked back up the hill.

I was home by 8pm.

On New Year's Eve.

The temperature had really dropped the past few days and it was a particularly chilly night. I lit a fire in the fire pit, made a cup of tea and sat on the terrace, wrapped up in blankets. There was a bottle of Trader Joe's Prosecco in the refrigerator, but I really wasn't in the mood. There were four hours left of what had been a really shitty year and I didn't feel like celebrating.

I watched the first round of fireworks go off across the city, and the twinkling headlights of traffic backed up along Sunset like an illuminated blocked artery.

If this was a movie, I suddenly thought, this magical view would be the backdrop to the two romantic leads sharing their first kiss. For the first time all day, I actually felt sad that I had no one to share it with.

Sunset Boulevard. I knew every inch of it so well: twenty-four miles of road stretching from Downtown to the Ocean.

At its origin, under the intersection of the Harbor (110) and Hollywood (101) Freeways, it's not quite sure if it wants to belong to the steaming kitchens of Chinatown or the glamour of the Mark Taper Forum and Disney Hall. It's kind of lost between them with vast apartment buildings flanking its source. Since it is born out of César Estrada Chávez Avenue, perhaps it owes its heritage more to southern California's Mexican ancestors.

From Downtown, Sunset Boulevard winds up in a north-westerly direction, past the Dodger Stadium and into Echo Park, home of the real artists, the painters, the designers, the musicians. They originally rented in Silver Lake but couldn't afford to buy there after the James Francos and Chris Pines and Ryan Goslings moved in, so they bought in Echo Park, which is just as nice and actually closer to the freeways. Because many residents own their homes there's a sense of pride in the area, which you might not quite pick up on as you pass the run-down strip malls and long frescos of graffiti art. You get a few hipsters moving in, but they usually try it out for a year and then move back to Venice.

There's a particular Spanish feel in the stretch between Echo Park and Silver Lake, where you'll also find the

Mexican drag queens and their karaoke bars. Stop for tacos at any one of the stands, and definitely grab a coffee at Café Tropical, which will be way better than the overpriced sludge they serve at Intelligentsia, I promise you. But everything else about Sunset Junction (where Santa Monica Boulevard starts and veers off in a westerly direction), which we are passing now, is wonderful. This is home to one of the first vegan cafés, Flore, which is nestled amongst the vintage shops and an army surplus store. Check out the thrift stores and the bakeries and Casbah café (a kind of Moroccan Central Perk) if it's still there. Fandango's hair salon, housed in a bright blue single storey Art Deco building, is just across the road there.

Now we're heading – still travelling northwest – through Los Feliz. There's Malo, home of the best margarita north of the Mexican border, and El Cid, where you can always catch a good band, and here's the Vista, a movie theatre built in 1923 that has retained its original façade. Now the road splits so make sure you're in the correct (left hand) lane otherwise you'll end up on Hollywood Boulevard to the north. Sunset heads due west now and everything gets a little clinical with medical centres on both sides of the street. That Kaiser Permanente building on your right unfortunately hides Barnsdall Art Park, so you can't see Frank Lloyd Wright's Hollyhock House but pay a visit if you've the time another day because it's really impressive.

A quick glance now at the imposing "Scientology Center" before we whizz through Thai town and find ourselves in a kind of wasteland full of more strip malls and endless beige apartment buildings before we head under the 101 Freeway, which we've finally caught up with since we left it Downtown and it looped down to the south of us. Now, as we continue west, the 101 heads north to cut through the Hollywood Hills.

Ah, *now* we've hit the real iconic landmarks. There's the KTLA radio tower, and on your left is Sunset Gower Studios. That white dome coming up on the left is the top of the Arclight movie theatre, and next door is one of my favourite places in Los Angeles: Amoeba Records. And now we're in the thick of Hollywood and there's the Hollywood Athletic Club, the Cat N' Fiddle pub, and all the famous strip clubs, some advertising that they have "totally nude girls". This is real Hollywood, the place, not the industry. There are no stars on the sidewalks of Sunset Boulevard; a lot of people don't realize that the walk of fame is confined to Hollywood and Vine.

It's all been a little seedy up to this point, and it remains so for a stretch, with countless bars, restaurants, tourist shops, eateries and discount shoe stores. And now here's a few more strip clubs, all conveniently close to Hollywood High School, the back of which continues for a whole block here before we hit In-N-Out, California's favourite burger joint, if you're into burgers.

Between La Brea and Fairfax, Sunset spruces itself up a bit. The restaurants get a little fancier, and there's the famous Guitar Center, and Samuel French (the British theatre bookshop) and Bristol Farms (the original fancy grocery store before Whole Foods took over the world, and where you can buy Marmite and other British goods if you can't make it down to the English Shop in Santa Monica). And over there is Kinkos.

After the Sunset Five complex, where you'll find Laemmle's Sunset 5 movie theatre, a Crunch gym and a Wolfgang Pucks, unless they've all moved on. There's also a coffee place and depending on what year you're in, it could be a Starbucks, a Coffee Bean, a Pete's or the general manager's office.

And now we are into serious Hollywoodland (the "town" not the place). *This* is where it has all happened. There's the Chateau Marmont hotel, where John Belushi died, and Jim Morrison nearly died, and Lindsay Lohan reportedly spent nearly $50,000 on room service. Right beside the hotel is the site of the original "Marlboro Man" billboard. He was replaced by an iPhone (I think) in the 90s, and his spot has gone to the highest bidder every year since.

Now we are in the heart of the Sunset Strip and you can run the gamut of the fanciest Hollywood hotels. Take a moment to marvel at the beauty of the iconic art deco Sunset Tower Hotel (where I once had average sex with a minor movie star in the penthouse suite during its previous incarnation as the Argyle Hotel). There's the Hyatt, the Standard, the Best Western Sunset (probably the cheapest room on the strip, at around $150 a night), the Mondrian and many more. And of course here we also have many famous clubs and bars. You've got the House of Blues, the Saddle Ranch (where I once fell off a bucking bronco), Mel's Diner (open 24 hours and where I once contemplated suicide at 4am after a huge fight with my best friend), and the Comedy Store (where I never once performed). And – pay attention now because they go by quick – there's the Billboard Club, the Red Rock, the Whisky a Go Go club and the unimpressive Viper Room where River Phoenix died.

Right after Doheny Drive, it's a very different story. We are on the northern border of Beverly Hills, at the southern foot of the Hollywood Hills and *now* we are in the money.

Most of these houses have private security guards and at least two pools. The 80-foot palm trees that line the streets are perfectly manicured and aligned. You've seen this stretch in countless movies and if you're ever in town over the holidays or during Halloween, it's worth a tour because these people try to out-do each other with their outdoor decorations.

But before it all gets a bit too "Stepford", the area gets a little more rustic and the road starts to wind around some pretty sharp corners and you might even find yourself leaning into the bend like you're on a motorbike. The road surface is beautifully smooth at this point, not a bump in sight, so it's a pleasure to drive. But you're not alone, there are plenty of other cars on the road, and the traffic is flowing fast, and everyone else has driven this stretch a thousand times so keep up and hold on tight because it's like a slipstream so *concentrate*, please, we don't need another car wrapped around a tree on the corner of Beverly Glen. We want you to be conscious and still driving by the time you're passing UCLA so you can marvel at the sheer size of the campus. A few more hairpin bends and it's all a little dull for a while as we pass the hermetically sealed properties of Bel Air, where all you will see are tall, solid gates and even taller hedges.

Finally, we've reached the 405 and you will see a prominent white building sticking out above the tree line, high up in the hills to the west of the freeway; this is the Getty museum but we're not going up there today.

We're cruising through Brentwood now. Just to your left is South Bundy Drive, where someone killed Nicole Brown Simpson in 1994, and over on your right is Rockingham Drive, where OJ Simpson lived at the time. Oh, I forgot to point out my old apartment building on the corner of Sunset and Barrington, the first place I ever lived in L.A.; that's okay, it was nothing special. I picked Brentwood because I felt safe there. Los Angeles is vast and utterly overwhelming when you first arrive, and Brentwood is a kind of scaled-down Beverly Hills where there are nice properties and manicured lawns, but without the extortionate price tags.

Moving swiftly on now and you can tell we've arrived in the Pacific Palisades because everyone is suddenly incredibly polite; they drive politely, they cross the street politely and they smile at each other a lot. It's all quite disconcerting considering we're on the west side. There are nice stores, plenty of cafés if you need to stop to pee – we've been in the car a long time, but don't take long because we're almost at the best part.

As Sunset approaches the beach there's a gorgeous little area that I like to call Poor Man's Malibu. It's not Malibu (which is just a bit further north up the coast), it's technically still the Palisades, but it has this real "beach community" feel. The houses (though worth $2 million plus) are tiny. These are the "beach houses" that I dream of. Or "beach shacks" might be a more accurate description, even though they're not technically on the beach (Yup, $2 million won't even buy you beach front in this part of the world!)

And now, ladies and gentlemen... a reverent hush, and then a little drum roll please... because *we... have... arrived*!

Yes, we are at Gladstones, the fish restaurant on the beach at the very end of Sunset Boulevard, where it meets the Pacific Coast Highway. We're going to park in the Gladstones parking lot. We'll grab a snack later, just to get the validation, but hurry up now because there's no time to lose. We don't want to miss one second of the stunning sight that is this epic boulevard's namesake.

The sunset.

We're out of the car now and we're walking onto the beach and there it is. There is the sun sinking into the vast Pacific Ocean. Look at that! And we've removed our shoes now and we're walking through the warm sand and now here we are at the water's edge. We throw down our shoes, roll up our jeans, and walk onto the wet sand where the foamy waves wash over our feet, and we cup our hands around our mouths and we shout out to the horizon,

"Hello Japan! Hello Tomorrow!"

Huddled up on the Adirondack chair, high up on the tree-house terrace, I watched the next wave of fireworks pop up – from this distance simply little clusters of sparks smaller than my fist – as the last few minutes of the year slipped away.

"Oh, L.A.," I sighed out loud. "I do love you."

And in that moment, I really, dearly wished L.A. would say it back to me.

Just once.

"It's no use going back to yesterday, because I was a different person then."

Alice's Adventures in Wonderland,
Chapter 10

LEWIS CARROLL

CHAPTER FIVE

The Girl Who Had Sex With Herself

"Do you need batteries to go with that?"

A month or so went by before I realized that something was missing in my relationship. It was Max who put the idea in my head.

January is always a productive time of year for me. I detox completely and get all sparkly and clear-headed. This year I had the added benefit of being smoke free. I was doing well on that front. Some days I didn't even think about it once. I hadn't had a Red Vine since Christmas Day (when I'd eaten them all).

I was ready to pitch my feature film idea to someone. My first someone for any new idea was usually Max.

I'd known Max through all three of my L.A. incarnations. We went way back. For five minutes, back when he was an assistant at CAA, I'd been higher up the food chain, but he was an ambitious shark and soon eclipsed me. Having flitted in and out of the studio system for several years, rising up the ranks rapidly, he was now a manager for a small but extremely cool and ultra powerful (on account of their niche client list) boutique management and production company.

What I liked about Max was his loyalty and honesty. He could be pretty brutal but at least he never yanked your chain. And he believed Hollywood was, and should remain, a meritocracy; that, despite it being show *business*, without the good material and the talent to portray it, there would *be* no business. He had the greatest respect for all artists… for writers, directors, actors, designers. He didn't care if you'd won an Oscar last year or had gotten off the bus from Ohio that morning, if the talent was there, if the material was good, he would get behind it.

Max's weakness was women. He'd screwed up at least three relationships with really great women because he could not keep his dick in his pants. I'd had a very brief dalliance with him when we'd first met. My memory was sketchy around the event, but there was a very high profile industry party. We were in a fancy hotel. We stole two bottles of champagne and broke into the spa at 2am. We managed to get the hot tub going and that's where things got bubbly and my recollection gets blurry. At some point we must have transferred to the loungers around the plunge pool. That's where the cleaner found us at 6am – covered in our clothes and the half dozen towels we'd taken from the reception area.

The occasion had been the culmination of weeks of flirting. We mutually agreed that, on account of the fact that we'd always associate any sexual activity with each other with the blinding hangovers we'd suffered the next day, we should quit while we were ahead. And we moved on to a decent, healthy Hollywood friendship. We had lunch about once or twice a year when I was in town. He had an unofficial "first look" at anything I wrote. So far, he'd shot everything down. But I enjoyed our lunches.

It was always entertaining to hear of his latest romantic pursuits. He wasn't a jerk, and he had huge respect for women professionally, he just wasn't cut out for monogamy, and he was slowly coming around to the idea that this was okay, as long as he was honest from the get-go and didn't get a girl's expectations up.

This time Max surprised me. Firstly, he did not shoot down my feature film concept. He thought it had real legs and told me to flesh it out and keep him in the loop. Secondly, he was full of excitement over the latest woman he'd met. She'd dragged him into therapy before they'd even consummated their relationship. He'd got to the bottom of why he was always sabotaging relationships. It was not because he was afraid of commitment but because he was afraid of being abandoned (his mother had died after a suspected intentional overdose of painkillers when he was 13) and if he screwed it up first, he could get out before falling in love and then getting his heart broken.

So far, he'd been with the girl for nearly nine months (they only finally started sleeping together three months into the relationship) and hadn't cheated, or even been temped.

I was genuinely happy for him.

"So what about you," he asked me finally. "I mean as far as men… seeing anyone? You were a mess after the break-up. You look better."

"Thanks," I smiled, pushing two rogue grains of rice against the side of my bowl with my chopsticks. I was going to get them into my mouth if it was the last thing I did. We were in our favourite sushi place on La Brea, just south of Wilshire, close to Max's office. "Actually I've decided to stop dating men for a year. I am actually dating *myself*." The recalcitrant rice grains were on my chopsticks finally and making their way to my mouth when I realized what I'd said. Catching sight of the look on Max's face, I immediately regretted it. He would grab any excuse to make fun of me. He did it in a kind, almost brotherly way, but I'd learnt over the years not to give him ammunition.

Something told me I'd just given him the mother lode.

"You mean like you take yourself out on dates and send yourself flowers?" he asked, eyes shining.

Flowers? Hmm. Valentine's Day was approaching. I made a mental note.

"Oh, I'm not actually serious," I mumbled, desperate to shrug it off and move on. "It's just an excuse not to date anyone for a year. I'm just scared of getting hurt again."

"No. It's *genius*," Max said, leaning forward conspiratorially. "I think you should absolutely do it. I hope you're keeping a journal. *This* I want to read. It's kind of Bridget Jones Does It Without Darcy." One of the ways Max liked to tease me was to compare me to Bridget Jones at any opportunity.

"Wait!" Max suddenly exclaimed, his eyes widening and glowing as if a giant light bulb had come on inside his head. "What about *sex!*"

"No, I'm sworn off sex, too," I sighed. "No men for a year. I've made a pact with myself."

"*No*, I mean if you're dating your*self*, well… what about… sex," and he mimed a gesture no man should ever mime. Off my blank stare and burning cheeks he advised me, "I would say now's *definitely* the time for a visit to the Pleasure Chest."

★

Before he'd scored the kind of income that allowed him to live alone in his own apartment and then graduate onto his current abode (a stunning four-bedroom Tudor style home in Hancock Park that he completely ripped out and remodelled, with a pool, and a guest house bigger than my London flat, in which I'd once stayed for a week when I was on a short visit between official L.A. incarnations), Max had lived with Ana. He credited Ana with changing his life.

Ana was a stunning woman but Max never stood a chance with her... because Ana was only into girls. On a weekly basis she would come home with bags from the Pleasure Chest. She seemed to shop in the Pleasure Chest as often as the average person would visit their local grocery store. When Max quizzed her about the place, she explained that it was an emporium of sex accessories. From underwear to toys, and from DVDs to bondage gear, anything that couldn't be sold in a regular retail outlet was sold in there. Max had become obsessed, had introduced every girlfriend and potential girlfriend to the wonders of the establishment, and had been urging me to go for years. I always laughed it off, saying it definitely wasn't my scene.

But now he had a point.

I knew exactly where this place was; I'd driven past it about 100 times. After hugging Max goodbye and promising (with my fingers crossed behind my back) to document every moment of my self-dating year for him to read, I headed north.

I had never driven so slowly up La Brea. As I approached Santa Monica, the big choice loomed. Did I turn right to go home or left to go *there*?

I turned right.

But then right again on Highland.

And right on Willoughby.

And right on Fairfax, then right onto Santa Monica, and finally left into the parking lot of the Pleasure Chest.

My heart was beating like a boom box as I got out of my car. The closest I'd been to a vibrator was watching Charlotte get addicted to her "rabbit" on *Sex and the City*. Something felt terribly illicit about walking into a sex shop, especially *alone*!

I attempted to leave my fear in the parking lot and feigned a casual attitude as I walked through the tinted glass doors, trying to make out like I frequented such establishments on a daily basis. *Just pretend like it's Trader Joe's*, I told myself as I strolled in. But on entering my local Trader Joe's, I was greeted with an array of artfully displayed artisan breads, not an assortment of leather and PVC crotch-less knickers.

There was no safe direction for my gaze. Everywhere my eyes settled I saw something more shocking than in the last direction I happened to glance. I just kept walking... until I found myself in the back of the shop. On the floor in front of me, in a glass display box the size of a large dog kennel, was a contraption that looked like a glute master – a machine I'd used (maybe twice) in the gym, where you get on all fours and strap one foot into a harness with weights attached to it so that you can lift your leg behind you and work your glutes into tight buns of steel.

This (hardly gym-friendly) contraption had a dildo strapped onto some kind of lever that was operated by the handles so you could take yourself from behind, doggy style. It reminded me of the machine George Clooney's character makes in *Burn After Reading*, which he shows off to Frances McDormand. One of those scenes that you just can't un-see.

Mortified to have been caught even looking at such a device, I turned on my heels and marched back into the centre of the store where I hid in a middle aisle between displays of butt plugs and butt butters. This was turning into an educational experience.

I took a couple of deep breaths.

When I felt I had regained my composure, I looked around and saw some phallic shaped objects on a shelf on the far wall. I slunk towards them. And *finally* I saw something familiar. It was a "Rampant Rabbit" just like the one featured in *Sex and the City*. I smiled. But my relief was short-lived.

"Can I help you?"

I nearly jumped out of my skin. I spun around to find a cute, petite sales assistant smiling at me. She had long dirty blonde dreadlocks, a nose ring, and a tattoo of a lizard on her neck. She was wearing a leather tank top with long rips in it, offering the viewer glimpses of her red bra, and very short faded denim shorts. Although she was little, she had these incredible, muscular legs. I wondered if she was an athlete. She smiled at me… in a way only guys had ever smiled at me.

"Yes. No. Yes! I mean, I don't know. I think, I'm… um… getting this." I waved the Rabbit at her, enthusiastically, forgetting that my palms were now covered in sweat. The box flew out of my hands and narrowly missed her head as it crashed into a display of chocolate body paint. "OhmygodIamsosorry!"

She picked up the box and put it safely back on the shelf; clearly she did not consider me a worthy owner of such an exuberant item.

"Are you buying your first vibrator?" she asked gently. And suddenly I was 13 and in Marks & Spencer with my mother telling the entire shop floor that I was looking to get fitted for my first bra.

"Well... I..."

"Are you looking for something that gives more vaginal stimulation, clitoral stimulation or both?" she asked. I'd never heard a woman say words like that before and for a few moments I froze. Suddenly I was on stage in an Oscar Wilde play and I'd just forgotten my next line, which was bound to be something to do with cucumber sandwiches.

I looked around, frantically, and lunged towards another shelf, grabbing a black, shiny object off it. It looked like a large over-ripe avocado wearing a tight belt.

"Whataboutthisone?" I demanded, my mouth suddenly so dry, my tongue was in danger of sticking to the roof of my mouth.

"It's good," she drawled, reaching forward so that her arm brushed the side of my left breast. She lifted off the shelf a pink object that looked like a large lipstick. "But this one will definitely give you the strongest clitoral stimulation."

"I'll take it," I squeaked.

She took forever ringing up the sale at the cash register. Finally, she asked, "Do you need batteries to go with that?" and I nodded vigorously. She could have sold me a hot tub, life insurance and solar panels so eager was I to get the hell out of the place.

The pink object masquerading as a lipstick did not come out of its box, which did not come out of the bag, which did not come out of the trunk of my car, for almost two weeks.

On the 14th of February, I walked into Trader Joe's and got everything I needed for my Valentine's date. I kept it simple. A little pasta and pesto would be nice, and I knew my date *loved* toasted pine nuts, so I tossed a pack of those overpriced seeds into my cart. Mango sorbet (of course), and maybe a little dark chocolate, the *really* dark one, to have with coffee after dessert? Now to the wine. This would be a little tricky. Obviously no more Trader Joe's cheap crap. Though she was known to make do with any cheap shit on certain occasions, my date was undoubtedly a wine snob at heart.

It had to be French. I selected a Bordeaux, from the Haut-Médoc region (AOC).

I was all set.

As I approached the checkout, I noticed big bunches of red roses in large plastic containers and my heart felt suddenly heavy. The ex had been lousy at many things in the romance arena but he'd never, ever forgotten to buy me a bunch of red roses on Valentine's Day. I couldn't face it. I looked away from the flowers.

A split second later I looked back, reached over and grabbed a bunch.

As I was waiting for the smiley checkout guy (they are all smiley in Trader Joe's) to bag up my groceries, I felt okay. I could do this. There was nothing weird about this.

"Lucky guy," said the smiley checkout guy.

"No guy," I said with confidence.

"So sorry, my bad," smiled the checkout guy. "Lucky girl."

"No girl either," I said proudly. "Except for me."

The checkout guy gave me a puzzled look as he handed me my bags. He'd stopped smiling. I grabbed my bags and bolted for the exit, thanking my lucky stars I'd chosen to go to the West Hollywood store instead of my local one. I could now boycott this one and I'd never have to see that checkout guy again.

When I got home, all the bags came out of my trunk.

Yes… *all* the bags.

Can we pause for a moment here because I need to explain something. Sorry, I know it's bad timing because it sounds like it's all getting rather saucy and exciting (or maybe you're dying with embarrassment for me) but there's a reason for all this prudishness and fear.

A long, long time before this, in my last year at boarding school, we were playing the truth game. Masturbation was not something teenage girls spoke about then, and perhaps they don't speak about it now, I wouldn't know, but it was certainly a taboo subject in my day. Conversely the boys talked all day long about different techniques and the best accessories for their favourite pastime (we'd heard they'd tried everything from socks to banana skins).

So when Courtney Kaplan, an American girl who joined us for a year while her mother and father (respectively big film producer and big film director) were shooting a movie in England, admitted to participating in a little self-loving, we were flabbergasted. Furthermore, she said, she had regularly used *a vibrator*! She claimed to have it with her at school, hidden in a secret place, but most of us started to doubt the story, as she never produced it. But it was the reaction of Emily McBride during that truth game that I never forgot.

"You have to be *really* careful," she said. "My aunt told me that you can ruin your future sex life if you use them. Because a man can't ever compete, so he becomes of no use to you. So if you use one you can probably forget about ever getting married and having children."

We had all gasped while Courtney laughed.

We weren't a Catholic school, but Emily McBride was from a big Irish Catholic family and only later in life, when I met people who *had* gone to Catholic schools, did I hear stories designed to put the fear-of-God into girls that were even more extreme.

I knew it was all Catholic propaganda but I guess the impact of that moment in our teenage truth game had never quite left me. Well, I wasn't going to let Emily McBride's aunt ruin my sex life any longer.

I put the roses in water and, before I could chicken out, got the pink bullet out of its packaging and laid it on my bed with the pack of batteries beside it.

"And there you will stay for a little while longer," I told it, while I went to retrieve the Bordeaux from the groceries bag. I poured myself a large glass and drank most of it fairly quickly. I was feeling pretty tense, so I decided to take a bath. I ran it nice and hot, and lit the candles on the closet floor (this was not a romantic gesture, this was the only way of getting any light into the space).

Mmm, this is going to be lovely, I thought to myself as I topped up my wine. I put Radiohead on at top volume, put my wine glass and the bottle beside the bath, and got in. The bathtub was so small you had to sit in it with your knees almost against your chest, but it was deep, so I was in hot water up to my neck. And I'd used a good amount of bubble bath, so there were loads of bubbles, and the flickering candle flames reflected off the white foam, making it all rather magical.

"My baby's got the bends…" I sang along with Thom York as loud as I wanted, confident that I was not disturbing anyone, shut away as I was in my bath-in-the-closet, in my little treehouse, at the top of a hill, in my little corner of heaven, where no one could see me, or know what I was going to do, thank you very much.

"Just lying in a bath…" I paused. It was "bar" not "bath"

"Making myself laugh…" I improvised, laughing. *"Waiting for something to happen."* I stopped laughing. *"I wish that something would happen."* I joined in randomly with the lines I vaguely knew.

"Where do we go from here?" I stopped singing and just drank my wine, suddenly feeling a little melancholy.

Halfway through 'Nice Dream', I realized I'd drunk most of the wine and the water was getting cold. I got out and wrapped my shrivelled body in a towel.

Maybe it was all that headbanging during 'The Bends' combined with the heat combined with the wine, but I was super dizzy when I got out of that bath. I lay down on my bed and tried to bring into focus a pink object lying beside me.

"Okayyy you… you *thing*, you weird pink thing," I slurred as I fumbled with the pack of batteries. I'd more skilfully opened condoms when drunk than the mess I was making of this packet. I got a little corner of the cardboard off, but then the plastic was so tight around the batteries, it was not budging. I finally used my teeth and gnawed the thing until I freed up two AAA batteries.

Nothing about this scenario felt in the least bit sexy, plus 'Bulletproof' was now killing the mood somewhat, but I soldiered on.

After several failed attempts, I got the batteries the right way up into the two little cavities. I turned it on. Damn thing made such a racket – even over the music – I swiftly turned it off again. Not sure exactly who I was trying to hide from (perhaps Thom York, which was fair enough), I closed my eyes for a second.

When I woke up, just before 4am, several questions bombarded my aching brain at once. First: why am I freezing? Second: what is this piece of cold plastic I'm clutching in my hand? And third: how fast can I run to Silver Lake Reservoir? Because *that's* how much water I need to get into my body, *right now*.

As I ate the pasta and pesto (with toasted pine nuts) I'd forgotten to cook the night before for breakfast, I took a solemn oath *never* to tell Max that I had failed to perform on what was supposed to be my big consummation night.

I also decided to give myself a second chance at giving myself a decent Valentine's date that night. But maybe I'd take myself *out* for dinner and give any battery-operated toys a wide berth.

My second favourite restaurant in the neighbourhood, after Café Stella, was barbrix on Hyperion Avenue. They had a big square bar in the middle of the space and did small plates of Mediterranean-style food, tapas style. The Argentinian owner had once been the Wine Director at Campanile so the wine list was exceptional. I had been thinking for a while that it might be the perfect location for my next attempt at a proper date with myself.

Plus it was the night after Valentine's. I'd be safe from cooing couples.

As I walked in, my heart sank a little. Clearly half the neighbourhood had decided to push Valentine's by one night and I hadn't got the memo. Every table had a cooing couple at it. And there were more at the bar. However, I'd remembered my book. Eckhart Tolle and I had failed to make much progress since December. I planned to push through the "pain body" chapter with renewed determination.

I found a free bar stool at one of the corners of the square bar and sat down, burying my head in the menu and trying my best not to look like one half of a lopsided couple… or a girl with an imaginary boyfriend.

I had a quick chat with the bartender and ordered a couple of dishes along with a glass of a white wine he recommended to pair with them, and then opened my book. Before I started to read I took a quick look around the bar, and as I was about to turn my attention back to my book, my eyes finally fell on the couple right across the corner of the bar from me, virtually next to me. Their faces were mashed together so I didn't see a face at first, but then the girl with her back to me, with the long blonde hair, pulled out of the kiss for a second and I saw the girl she was kissing.

It was ice girl from New Year's Eve.

"Hiiii," I trilled as if she was a friend I'd known for years, before wishing the ground would open up and swallow me. She looked at me blankly. "You work at that restaurant on Sunset, right?" I went on. "At Maltman. I was there on New Year's Eve."

There was an excruciating pause.

Finally the ice girl spoketh.

"Okay," she said blankly, humouring me. Her girlfriend now turned to look at me. She was ridiculous. She looked like Charlize Theron. And looked *at* me like I'd farted.

"Yes, I didn't stay very long," I wittered on. "But remember you made me a strawberry daiquiri? And I told you I was on a date with myself, that I was dating *myself*? Well, here I am, six weeks later. I made it to Valentine's with myself. Yay me!"

Have they named this condition yet? The one that makes you say the most embarrassing things, and you can't shut up and the worse it gets the more you keep digging? I wish they would hurry up. I need an official diagnosis. And a cure!

Ice girl gave me the smile you might give someone who has, literally, days left to live. It was almost kind in its level of pity. Charlize's expression was more, "Why don't you leave right now and do us all a favour." Without missing a beat, she quickly turned back to her icy lover and locked their lips together again, somehow managing to cover both of them with her golden mane of hair, as if drawing a curtain across a private event.

The next day I officially cancelled Valentine's Day.

Forever.

Without any intention of speaking to him directly (*obviously*), I considered what Max would have told me do in my dilemma.

"Not getting any at home, buddy, what do you suggest?" I asked him, in a deep, manly "bro-to-bro" kind of voice in my imaginary conversation. I knew exactly what Max, *old* Max at any rate, would have told me to do.

I had never "played away". Never. Okay, there was a backstage kiss with an actor who was my co-star in a pretty raunchy play we'd been cast in on the Edinburgh Fringe when I was still *technically* with my first boyfriend. But the fires had long gone out between that boyfriend and me, and the writing was on the wall, and four weeks later we were over anyway.

I genuinely did not understand the point of cheating. I once knew a couple who decided to have an "open relationship". I believe many couples do. They were the only straight couple I knew personally who tried it. Many gay couples I know do it quite successfully, with really strict rules like "never in the marital bed" and "never with the same guy twice". For some reason, perhaps societal conditioning based on religious precepts that don't hamper the gay community, women aren't as understanding of their partner's inability to turn down a once-in-a-lifetime chance of a threesome on the opening Friday of a business conference when he's staying in an all-expenses-paid five-star hotel in Hawaii and has been drinking champagne all afternoon with two twenty-five-year-old female entrepreneurs who are single and loaded – in every conceivable sense.

The couple I knew who tried it were divorced within 12 months.

Before that, I'd thought it was just the *dishonesty* that destroyed people. Like how devastated Max's fiancée had been when she came home early from a work trip and found him in their bed with his intern. The worst part of it was that she didn't do any drama. She didn't speak to him… in fact she never spoke a word to him again. She just packed up her things and left, sending friends and a removals team around the following week for everything else. Max let her have anything she wanted. She took everything… except the bed. He had to start again from scratch. I'd gone furniture shopping with him after a lunch we had shortly after the incident. I think that was the one that hit home and it was probably half the reason the current girl-friend had been able to get him into therapy. Sadly, the ex fiancée hadn't been able to shake the depression that set in. She'd taken so much time off work she lost her job. No one knew what happened to her after she moved back to Nebraska to live with her sister's family. She'd cut everyone from social media. The guilt nearly destroyed Max, too.

So if you got permission, it was still a risk. So what should you do if you ask permission and your other half says, "Sure. Go ahead."?

Well, there was only one way to find out. I asked myself for a hall pass. I said,

"Sure. Go ahead."

"Curiouser and curiouser!" cried Alice (she was so much surprised, that for the moment she quite forgot how to speak good English)...

Alice's Adventures in Wonderland,
Chapter 2

LEWIS CARROLL

CHAPTER SIX

The Girl Who Cheated on Herself

*Cheating is the best way of avoiding the real
problem. It's like going out for ice cream
when the roof starts leaking.*

I missed kissing. I *loved* kissing. There were many things I could do with myself whilst dating myself (even if in some activities I had, so far, only scored a "must try harder"), but kissing was certainly not one of them. I could take myself out for dinner, I could buy myself gifts and flowers, I could die of embarrassment in sex shops, but I couldn't enjoy the delights of exploring another mouth with mine, of pushing my lips against another pair of lips, of debating why noses had been designed with no regard for kissing at all.

Yes, I was a big fan of kissing. And I felt rather bereft without it in my life. Indeed, I would take good kissing over mediocre sex any day. *Good* kissing, mind. There is nothing so unpleasant as bad kissing.

When we were 16, Amber (my unofficial best friend at boarding school) and I made a list of all the boys we'd kissed so far. Some girls were having sex by then but we genuinely had no interest in the other sex acts on the menu.

Yes, there was a menu.

Before you'd had any sexual activity of any kind, you were 100% innocent. French kissing (proper snogging with tongues) knocked 10% off your score. So you became 90% innocent once you'd done that. Having your boobs felt up over clothes knocked off 10%; under clothes was a further 10% gone. You lost 10% of your innocence if you got fingered, and another 10% for giving a blowjob, another for doing a 69. And so it went on. I have genuinely forgotten what the last two were before actual penetration but I don't think I've ever heard of them since so I'm pretty sure I'm still 20% innocent to this day.

Amber and I were both at 50% and quite happy to stick at that. We'd had more or less identical experiences. We'd both suffered the discomfort of having the fingers of a drunken teenage boy prodding around our barely nubile vaginas. We'd both had our heads pushed down onto an erect penis without any warning. Lucky for me, it happened to Amber first so she was able to warn me to breathe through my mouth somehow, to avoid getting a whiff of stale urine. "Suck, then take a breath; suck, then a breath." Neither of us was keen to try it again.

But kissing was *great*. We considered ourselves judges in the kissing Olympics.

Our scoring system was quite straightforward. We had four categories: Looks, Personality, Sexiness, Kissing Technique. We scored them out of ten in each category and then they got an overall score, but the only *really* important score was the one for kissing technique. A boy could be forgiven for being fairly ugly, having a boring personality and absolutely zero obvious sex appeal if he was a great kisser.

By the time we had both kissed 20 boys, Amber had found two "9"s. I had one "10" but I also had a "0". I had to give him a "0". Amber agreed with me, on account of his actions, too.

He was 24 when I was 13. He was actually my first ever proper kiss and it's lucky it didn't scar me for life. (Or perhaps it did.) It was at my older cousin's wedding. He'd put the moves on me. He wasn't bad looking (a "7" I think) and I told him I was 16 (which I easily passed for at 13) because I really was desperate at that point to get off the starting blocks. Only one other girl in my year was still 100% innocent and she had railway-track braces on her teeth so she had a decent excuse.

Anyway, this guy took me outside, walked me across the golf course (where the reception was being held), pushed me down on the grass and then started to grind his face into mine. He practically *ate* my mouth. His "five o'clock shadow" scratched my lips and chin to pieces. I had a rash for a week. His tongue was *huge* and he pushed it so far into my mouth I choked on it, which at least stopped the kissing for a moment. I said I had to go to the loo. He told me to go in the bushes. I told him it was a "number two" which thankfully repulsed him… so much he let me go inside. Otherwise, who knows what might have happened.

I spent the rest of the wedding avoiding him and dancing with the younger children where I felt safe.

The quality of men and kissing got better over the course of my teenage years – with a few notable exceptions – and by the time I was into my early twenties and had embarked on my first long-term relationship (I was quite a late bloomer on that front) I *did* get into all the other things you can do with a boy. But I definitely believe you can learn all you need to know about your compatibility with someone in their kisses.

Good kissers are all good in their own unique way. Bad kissers more or less fall into one of three categories: grabbers, dribblers and moaners.

You can tell you've got a grabber just before he kisses you, but when it is unfortunately already too late. He grabs the back of your head, or your face. Or if he's a real expert he gets one whole arm around your back to pin you to his body and uses the other hand to hold your head in place while he plants his mouth tight as a suction cup on yours. He mashes his face into yours and leaves you looking like you took a piece of sandpaper to your mouth. I find aloe gel is very soothing in these instances.

The dribblers just have the most unbelievable amount of excess saliva. What is it with guys and excess saliva? Is this why they need to spit? I am pretty sure I've never seen a woman spit in the street and I've always been disgusted when I see men do it, but maybe it's a genuine medical problem. Can't they just swallow it? Mind you I don't like it when it's all in my mouth and I don't want to swallow it, so maybe I need to give these guys a break. Okay, guys, carry on as you were, spitting in the street. But get rid of it before kissing, please.

The moaners are not necessarily bad at the actual physical activity of kissing but the moaning and grunting that comes with it is so off-putting, they're really not worth it.

Having said all of this, my aunt swears that my uncle was absolutely hopeless at kissing. But over the years she trained him to kiss well. They were married for thirty years. Sadly, he had a fatal heart attack when he was 64. A few years after he died, my aunt felt ready to date again. She was only a youthful 62. However, she said she would only consider men who kissed exceptionally well. She wasn't giving any bad kissers a second thought; they would be discounted on contact. She didn't have time to train another one.

Really exceptionally good kissers are rare. I've had a few and they've been hard to quit, even when everything else about them isn't really up to scratch. A fantastic kisser is highly addictive.

Keanu was just such a kisser.

My friend Molly had worked for an events company for ten years. Event organizers and all associated businesses do very well in Hollywood. There's always another premiere or awards ceremony or company holiday party. They are all trying to out-do each other so spend ever increasing amounts of money. And they spend even more when they hit rough times.

Like the aging actor guy.

Molly had been hired to do a party for this guy once; he was an aging actor. After a massive hit TV show in the 1980s, he hadn't been in anything for years. He apparently spent a lot of money of women and drugs. His wife caught him one too many times and filed for divorce. She had practically been his free personal assistant and manager for years. He went on a massive spending spree to drive himself into bankruptcy before a settlement could be awarded to his wife and threw the most ridiculous party. It was a costume party and he set up a tab at this costume rental place so everyone could rent whatever costumes they wanted; no expense spared. There were white horses dressed up as unicorns. There were live flamingos shipped in from Florida. There were chocolate fountains the size of real fountains – several people fell into these and ruined their costumes, so the deposits were lost on those. An entire igloo was built, inside of which everything was made of ice; even vodka shots were served in cups made out of ice.

Of course, Molly's company didn't know the extent of the debt the guy was in by then. They went ahead and did the whole party and then found out he couldn't pay the final bill (which was almost the U.S. average annual salary).

In the end the ex-wife, who had invested plenty of money in her own name, paid it. I hope she at least got a ride on a unicorn.

Molly was a workaholic. She lived life in a bubble; a work bubble. If you wanted to see Molly, you had to see her at work, which wasn't such a bad deal.

This event was the launch of a minor celebrity's gin brand at the Mondrian hotel, which is home to the famous Skybar. She left me a message out of the blue asking me to come, telling me my name was on the door with a plus four, begging me to bring girls. The celebrity's guest list was almost all male and the PR company was demanding Molly even out the numbers. She promised me I'd know people there, but she always promised me this, and I never did, I'd ducked out of the Hollywood scene years ago.

And so, for the first time in months, I ventured out into public. I parked six blocks away to avoid the valet risk, almost at Fountain and Crescent Heights, and walked in flats, carrying my heels in my bag. It was such a relief knowing I could come back to my car and it would as I'd left it, in Neutral.

When I got to the Skybar I waited patiently in line, gave my name on the door, explained there was no plus anyone, walked through onto the terrace and took my gin cocktail from a tray offered by a waiter. I could see Molly in the DJ booth giving a moody looking DJ instructions. I managed to catch her eye and waved. She gave me a quick wave back. This was probably the closest I'd get to her all night.

I looked around at all the beautiful women and men – mannequins for the fashion industry. They all looked like they were inflicted with wandering eye syndrome as they talked to one person but looked in another direction to check whether there was someone more important to talk to nearby. There was a time when I would have given my left arm to be on the guest list for a party like this because I thought with status came security. But as I edged my way up the Hollywood food chain I discovered that status was actually *inversely* proportional to security. Some of the most powerful players in town were hooked on pills to manage their anxiety disorders. I had steered away quickly.

But once in a while I came along to one of these events for fun, to remember what the view was like in this mad world, to remind myself that I was perfectly happy existing on the outskirts of it.

I looked around for somewhere to sit and have an imaginary cigarette, and remembered the only bad thing about the Skybar was the provision of seating. The only place to sit down was on these vast white mattresses dotted about the place and around the pool. They were about six inches off the ground and impossible to get onto or off of in anything resembling a dignified manner. Why had I worn my too-tight jeans? As I scolded myself internally, I knelt on the corner of a giant cushion that already had four or five people sprawled across it and then managed to roll to one side to get into a half reclined position, leaning back on my elbows.

"Excuse me," I turned my head to see Keanu Reeves kneeling beside me. Well it wasn't Keanu Reeves (I don't think, I couldn't swear) but he was a dead ringer for him. "Do you have a light?" Keanu asked.

"Sorry, I don't smoke," I smiled at him and held up my right hand with my index and middle two fingers pointing up. "This is just an imaginary cigarette."

Keanu laughed.

"Trying to quit?"

"No, I *did* quit," I said in a very serious tone. "There is no try." Keanu threw back his whole head as he laughed. He looked at me and his eyes lit up.

"Once you start down the dark path, forever will it dominate your destiny, consume you it will," he said in a perfect impression of the pint-sized Jedi Master. Seriously, maybe it really was Keanu (but straight off the set of *Point Break*, having arrived through a time tunnel from 1991).

"I'm not actually a *Star Wars* geek," I confessed. "I just know a few of the most famous quotes and scenes. But I know that was an excellent Yoda."

"Thank you." He smiled at me. I noticed a woman on the next cushion was smoking. "That woman's smoking if you want a light."

"I don't smoke, either," Keanu revealed. "It was just a line." I felt my cheeks go warm.

"What would you have done if I'd said I had a light?" I asked him.

114

"Ask you for a cigarette."

"So you would have *started* smoking if I'd been a smoker?"

"Whatever it takes to get to talk to a pretty girl."

"Ugh!" I groaned. "That is a terrible line. You were doing so well. You've just lost all your points."

"Damn!" he whispered, moving closer to me. "Can I try and win some back?" He brought his head closer to mine and I felt like I'd been plugged straight into an electrical socket. He was just oozing sexual charisma. The gin was kicking in and going to my head. Or was I being intoxicated by the heat coming off this guy?

Then he kissed me. Man, it was an awesome kiss. Just one kiss, a light touching of the lips. Hello! More o' that, please. I went in for more, dropping my imaginary cigarette on the floor as I buried my fingers in his hair, mirroring him as he now had his hands behind my head. I swung my legs – somehow elegantly – over his. Suddenly everything was effortless. It was like we were in a scene from a movie.

Soon, we were lip-locked in La La Land.

Who knew cheating could feel so good?

Finally we pulled apart for a breather.

"You know I really shouldn't be doing this," I said. "I'm kind of in a relationship with someone." I was about to tell him about my mad dating quest because it did seem to amuse the boys, but before I could continue he said, grinning and flashing his left hand at me, "So am I."

Ugh! How had I missed the wedding ring?

I excused myself immediately and made a beeline for the exit, making a mental note to be more discerning about which of Molly's generous invitations to accept. I'd stick to the small brunches and spa launches. I'd leave the Hollywood glitz, glamour and shmucks to the younger generation. Time to pass the baton.

I felt a little short changed by my dalliance. Could a quick, booze-fuelled kiss at a high profile party really be classified as cheating? I thought of Keanu's wife. I'm sure I knew how *she'd* classify it, but I still felt like I hadn't used my "get out of jail free" card.

Which is maybe why I found myself a little more dressed up than usual, wearing a little more make-up than usual, at barbrix the following Saturday night.

I took a seat at the bar, ordered a glass of wine and found myself seated next to a small odd-numbered group. There was a girl and a guy who were clearly a couple. And then there was Steve Martin. He looked like a young Steve Martin.

And as luck would have it, he was as funny as Steve Martin. Making me laugh can go a long way and make up for a lot of points lost in the looks department. By the end of the night I was pretty smitten.

He asked for my number.

"Are you married?" I asked without hesitation.

"Not when I last looked," he said. "But I'll check again as soon as I get home."

"Seriously," I said. "No partner, no girlfriend."

He reassured me he was single.

I gave him a light kiss on the lips, said, "Call me," and left.

As I walked home I wondered what felt so different about that exchange with Steve. Well, it wasn't as intense as my usual encounters for a start. Because I wasn't *that* attracted to him, I didn't care *that* much whether he called or not. I was used to so much drama, the headiness of mind-blowing kissing, or sex; or the promise of sex, and then the huge disappointment. The obsessing over whether a guy was going to call, the rush of starting a new relationship, the passion within a relationship, the emotional fallout of the end of a relationship… all drama.

I didn't feel any drama over Steve.

I had given a guy my number. I was cool. I had no control over whether or not he called. I was cool. Wait a second, back up there…

I had *no control* over whether or not he called?

Suddenly I started obsessing over whether or not he would call.

Damn, I should have kissed him properly. Given him something worth calling for.

A week went by and Steve hadn't called. I decided it was time to hang out at barbrix again. Either I would run into him and could act all cool and nonchalant, or I'd meet someone else.

I met someone else.

This guy was a dead ringer for Seth Rogan. I only believed he wasn't because he showed me his ID, well… his CNN pass. He was a journalist. He'd won awards.

Now we're talking.

Seth and I chatted over a bottle of Chilean Carménère that the Argentinian had graciously allowed onto his wine list. Seth suggested we eat something.

"Are you okay with garlic?" he asked.

"If you are," I replied in coded agreement that we would end up kissing.

There was plenty of garlic at barbrix and a fair amount of kissing on the corner of Hyperion and Lyric Avenue where Seth had left his car (he lived in Glendale). He was a decent kisser. He promised to call me when he got back from a quick two-day trip to Mexico City where he was attending a NAFTA committee meeting.

So I was cool for two days, then three. By Day Four, he was close to using up the time I'd allotted him to unpack and get over the travelling. On Days Five and Six I decided he was very busy writing up the story for CNN. On Day Seven I ran out of excuses and the *real* obsessing started. I couldn't figure out why he wouldn't call. We had had the most fascinating conversation. We'd be great together. I mean I was only looking for a quick fling of course, no relationship, but… we'd be *great* together. Our kids would be so smart. I started planning the wedding.

Finally, on Day Nine, my phone rang.

It was Steve.

Steve took me to a microbrewery in Eagle Rock. He picked me up in his red 1986 Jaguar XJ6, his pride and joy. He was an Anglophile and wasn't impressed that I wasn't impressed with his car.

"I'm sorry but the only car that really impresses me is the Tesla Roadster," I said. I'd test driven it once. "And perhaps the Prius."

You don't say such things to a classic car enthusiast. It's like telling a Michelin-starred chef you're a vegan. They do what they do to impress you. How are they supposed to impress you if they can't show off their toys and skills?

We drove into an area I didn't know that felt like a bit of a wasteland. Fortunately, there was a brightly lit parking lot behind the bar.

Steve parked in the furthest corner of the lot.

"Let me get the door for you," he said. Taken aback by such chivalry, I waited until he got out, walked around to my side and opened the passenger door. I was barely upright when Steve grabbed my head with both hands and kissed me so hard I thought my lip would burst between the pressure of his teeth and mine.

"MMMMM," he moaned. "UMMMM, OOOOH!"

Keeping my head pinned to his with one hand, he used the other to pull down my loose-fitting dress and grab my boob.

"AAAARRR," he groaned.

It was only at this point that I realized how much saliva was running down my cheek. He was full of it; his mouth was pouring out saliva.

Great! He was a grabber, dribbler *and* moaner. Triple whammy!

What were the chances?

Using an age-old tactic, I managed to detangle my tongue from his long enough to say, "I really need to use the bathroom, can we go inside."

"Sure," Steve said, finally releasing me. He locked the car and as we walked to the bar, slapped my butt and said, "You're just *so* irresistible."

*

We drank beer for an agonising hour or so. Suddenly he wasn't so funny. An unfunny Steve Martin who is a terrible kisser is not really who you want to hang out with.

Finally, I said I had an early meeting and had to get home.

When he went to grab me again in the parking lot, I dodged out of the way and said my throat was suddenly really sore. He begged me to come home with him where he promised to make me honey and lemon. (Ahhh...) (No!)

I talked up the meeting. I said anything that came into my head. It was the meeting that could change my life, turbo-boost my career. I had to give a big pitch. I hadn't practiced my pitch enough. I'd suddenly been inspired and needed to write down some new ideas. I stopped short of claiming I was meeting Spielberg himself.

When he dropped me off I made sure I mentioned that I was going to be in New York for two weeks and was then moving out of the treehouse (in case he got any ideas). As soon as I got inside I blocked his number.

After the Steve incident I decided cheating was overrated. But just as I was deciding how to spice things up under Plan A, and make dating myself more interesting, I got the most exquisite kiss from the most unexpected source.

I had this group of fair-weather friends in Manhattan Beach. I say fair-weather not because they were flaky but because the weather is *always* fair in Manhattan Beach. They would invite me to parties occasionally. It was far enough away to stay over night in one of the many guest rooms in the eight-bedroom mansion they lived in and make it feel like a mini-holiday.

My original route into this group had actually been through Molly. She invited me to the baby shower for a British pop star married to a U.S. TV star (stretching the word "star" in both cases) at Inn of the Seventh Ray in Topanga.

"Sweetie I need a few more vegetarians to fill it out," she'd shouted at me over speakerphone from her car en route between meetings.

"But I'm—"

"And Paula Abdul will be there."

"In!" (*now* we are talking "pop star"!)

Paula Abdul was most definitely *not* there, unless she had an extraordinarily elaborate disguise, but the party was one of the best Molly had ever invited me to. The restaurant was like walking into some heavenly oasis. The food would have turned any carnivore into a vegetarian. And I met Star (her real name, ironically).

Star was loaded. And I mean probably not at a level you or I could comfortably conceive of. I didn't know that then, of course. At the time, she was just this stunning, ethereal spirit who happened to be seated at my table. She was an ageless beauty. You could have placed her anywhere between 30 and 50. We got talking about music. She said she had a studio in her house in Manhattan Beach and invited me to come jam with her some day.

She was lying. She didn't have a house; she had a palace. The place just went on and on. It didn't feel grand, it was incredibly homely, but it was simply huge. And it was one block from the beach, but all hidden behind a huge fence that was covered in greenery so you really felt like you were cut off from the world… until you went up onto one of the many roof terraces dotted around the third storey of the house and got the most breath-taking views of the Ocean and the whole panoramic sweep of Santa Monica bay from Point Dume to Palos Verdes.

In the basement was the recording studio and it surpassed even those I'd seen in movies. I couldn't quite believe that much equipment could exist in one place and I certainly had no idea what it all did. The first time Star gave me the tour and asked if I wanted to play something or work on a song with her, I was: *I don't think so*! I was far too nervous. I said I was honoured she'd asked me but that I wasn't feeling the creative juices flowing. I told her I'd try and work on something and then let her know when I was ready to workshop it.

I was still working on it.

You might assume that Star's house was crawling with celebrities, that she had record producers hanging around that basement, and an entire entourage. But she was completely fame-phobic and hung around a pretty close group of friends, most of whom were artists and musicians, or yoga teachers. Some were retired; I wasn't sure from doing what. They were all ages, and came from all places, but they all had one thing in common. They were all genuine and lovely, kind people. Some lived in the house, some lived near by, many were ex-roommates, some dropped by and stayed for a week on their way through from Chile back to India. They were, for some reason, quite enamoured with me and I had been to several parties there over the years. There was a little tension with Molly when she heard, and realized she was never invited, but I kind of understood why they didn't invite her. It really wasn't Molly's scene.

She would have called them all hippies, if she'd even taken the time out to drive out there. But she was mostly jealous because Star was a Somebody – or at least *considered* a Somebody by virtue of the fact she was loaded, knew everybody, but was shrouded in mystery and didn't play the Hollywood game.

Everyone was curious about Star's background. Molly had told me that there was once a rumour going around that Star was Jim Morrison's only living (proven) biological child and that the two beneficiary families (the Morrisons and the Coursons, who controlled the estate) had given her and her mother (since deceased) an enormous pay-out when Star had taken a DNA test in the late 80s. This had been laughed off by Star (who had never revealed the source of her income or the identities of her parents) but it was a great story, and had been passed around, and had turned into a real urban legend.

The party was in honour of Star's friends Charles and Indigo who had finally successfully adopted their first child from Laos. They had been trying for several years and had almost been successful several times. Now the baby was safely home with them and Star wanted to celebrate at the house. Charles and Indigo had been her roommates for a few years before they bought a place together. They were all like family.

I felt such a sense of peace and joy as I took the 101 to the 110 to the 105 to the 405 to Manhattan Beach. This was how I always felt when I went out there, as if the power of Star's positive energy reached me from 20 miles out and drew me in to harbour.

And the party was, as you'd expect, full of love and happiness for this new child. I got there just after 4pm and spent hours cooing over the baby and hearing the whole story about her journey into the world and into her new home. There were several people I hadn't seen for a year or more at the party, so I caught them up with what was going on with me… editing profusely.

It was interesting. In this crowd, amongst the people who were least likely to judge me, I gave away almost nothing.

How are things with you?

Oh good, thank you. (Not *I struggle to remember the point of living some days.*)

Are you still doing the long-distance thing with the British boyfriend?

No, that didn't work out, sadly. (Not *the bastard broke my heart out of the blue and I may never be with a man again as a result.*)

When are we going to see your TV show?

Hopefully soon, we're just at the end of the development process. (Not *the producers are fucking killing me with idiotic notes, so probably fall 2032. With any luck I might live to see it.*)

It wouldn't be right or fair to taint the upbeat spirit of these wonderful people.

By 10pm, Charles and Indigo had long gone, to take the baby home to bed, and a small group of us remained. I had been thoroughly enjoying the Caribbean punch that the neighbours had made and were serving out of huge tin tubs. I was now a little wobbly on my feet. I found Star lying on a giant beanbag by the pool and flopped down next to her.

"This has been such a special night. Thank you so much for inviting me!" I said, hoping I wasn't slurring.

"Of course," Star said in her syrupy voice that was as beautiful when she sang as when she talked. "I'm glad you were able to make it."

"I'm so happy for them," I sighed. "They've waited so long for this."

There was a pause. Star was looking at me intensely.

"What?"

"Tell me what's really going on, Jess. You're not fooling me with the breezy attitude."

I lay back and looked up at the night sky.

"Oh, I don't know. I'm just trying to figure life out. Trying to be okay with being single. And having my career in the dumpster. And probably never having children." I had to stop talking because I found myself getting all choked up on emotion.

"Hey," said Star, stroking my arm. "Don't say that. You can have whatever you want. You just have to let it in… not be afraid of letting it in."

I smiled at her. I never quite understood half of what Star said.

"I quit smoking," I said, suddenly.

"I noticed! Good for you!" she exclaimed, and offered me a high five. "You see… you're making positive, healthy changes."

"For what," I mumbled.

"For *you*."

I was doing my best not to full on cry and had been doing well until Star put an arm around me, snuggled into me and said, "You deserve good things. The best. And you'll get them. You just have to get out of your own way. You need to find a little more love for yourself."

★

When I'd finished having a little full-on cry, I propped myself up and looked at Star.

"You're so beautiful," I told her. "So kind and generous and caring and loving. Why are there no men like you?" And suddenly Star looked at me in a different way. It reminded me of a look someone had given me not so long ago... in a particular store somewhere... on Santa Monica and Fairfax.

I felt all tingly, especially at the top of my head.

"Why do you need me to be a man?" Star said, carefully. "Are you only into men?"

Well, you could have knocked me down with a feather... if I hadn't already been lying down.

"I think so," I said, in barely more than a whisper.

"Why don't you find out for sure," she suggested. Her face was now a couple of inches from mine and her intention was obvious. She didn't make a move, so I did. I went in for a kiss. I put my lips on hers and kissed her. And she kissed me back. Before I knew it I was kissing this beautiful woman, someone who was so kind and generous and caring and loving.

"Wow," I said, pulling back for a moment. "You're a *really* good kisser."

"It takes two," she said, pulling me back for more. And as we kissed I tried to recall seeing Star with a man and realized I hadn't.

"Wow," I said again, pulling back again.

"Are you okay," she asked, stroking my cheek.

"Yeah, it's just a little weird, you know..."

"Because you haven't kissed a woman before?"

I thought about it and answered truthfully. "I have actually. Twice. Well, they kissed me. Once was in a play. Well, not *in* the play, we were doing a play and we were waiting in the wings to go on and she suddenly grabbed me and started kissing me, and then we went on and I forgot my words. And the other time I was at dinner at this girl's house and her boyfriend came over and she suddenly started kissing me, saying her boyfriend wanted to watch us, and I quickly left. But this is the first time I... made the first move."

"And you haven't forgotten your words. And you haven't run away," Star said, smiling.

"Does this make me a lesbian?" I asked, tentatively. She laughed.

"You can call yourself anything you want. I don't believe anyone is all straight or all gay. I think we're all curious, sexual creatures. You might be more into one particular gender, but I think being with the other is *never* off the table if there's the right connection."

We kissed for a little longer before I suggested we go get another drink. After that, even though she was the hostess, Star never left my side. She entwined her fingers around mine. She stroked my back. She planted little kisses on my neck and cheeks. No one around us batted an eyelid. Not a judgemental crowd.

When I said I was tired and needed to go to bed, Star came with me. At the door of the bedroom I was sleeping in, I stopped and turned to her.

"I don't think I can, you know, go any further," I wasn't sure of many things in my life at that point, but I was sure I didn't want to get naked with Star. "You know I adore you and think you're the most incredible woman I've ever met. And you're beautiful and the *best* kisser, maybe the best I've ever had but," my eyes travelled down her body a little, her

127

beautiful, slender body. "I really couldn't do… anything else. I'm really sorry."

Star gave me a big smile, but it was the first time I'd ever seen anything resembling sadness on her face.

I slept on and off for a few hours, and at around 6am, when I was sure I was sober enough to drive, I crept through the silent house, let myself out of the garden gate, and walked the couple of blocks to my car.

As I drove home, I felt surprisingly sad. I wasn't sad that I wasn't a lesbian (although, damn, that was a hot woman I just turned down, could I not have just *tried it once, for fuck's sake!*) I was sad because I didn't feel the things that Star felt (again… *not the things she felt when she looked at a woman she had the hots for.*) I was sad because something was stopping me from feeling the joy she felt. And I had a feeling that something might be me.

I got home, had a hot shower and got into bed. As I dozed off I contemplated my conquests.

So… I'd successfully cheated on myself four times. (Well, three technically, because everyone knows… it doesn't count if it's with a woman.) But I was becoming painfully aware of the fact that I couldn't neglect my objective of dating myself forever.

And I'd discovered something else important… I had discovered exactly what cheating *is*: cheating is the best way of avoiding the real problem. It's like going out for ice cream when the roof starts leaking.

Maybe I needed to start fixing the leaking roof.

*

While I incubated my latest thoughts, I busied myself with finishing the latest round of dubious notes from the producers, writing a business plan for a friend in London, and browsing Craigslist for apartments. I had two weeks left in the treehouse. I took a break from dating altogether, me included. I didn't even think about dating for a while.

Star didn't call.

Which was a good thing. Although it stung a little.

The one issue that kept gnawing at me was what had happened on the beach when I'd tried to meditate. I was still trying to get my head around it. I usually failed to make much sense of it, so I'd push it out of my thoughts for a while. But it kept coming back.

What exactly happened?

What did I see?

What did it mean?

Should I try it again?

It was this last thought that really kept knocking on my skull. Really? Why? To be honest, the experience had frightened me a little. There was that moment when I couldn't hear any noises from the beach. I had convinced myself that I'd just momentarily fallen asleep. That was my explanation. That would do for me. But some little stubborn and curious bone inside me wouldn't let it go.

So one evening, after I finished making some appointments to see apartments the next day, I built and lit a fire in the fire pit and settled down on the terrace. As well as the two Adirondack chairs, there was a wooden bench. I reckoned that would make a better surface to sit cross-legged on.

I sat down and wiggled my butt around a little until it was not hideously uncomfortable. Why didn't I get a cushion?

So I got up and got a cushion from inside.

That was better.

I started again. I parked myself on the cushion and watched the fire, preparing to meditate. But I suddenly had a craving for a cup of tea. Yes, a cup of tea would be perfect first. Relax with a cup of tea.

I went into the kitchen, made my tea and brought it out to the deck. Then I watched the fire burn as I drank my tea.

I took the empty cup inside, came back out and settled down again.

I was just about to close my eyes when I suddenly thought it might be irresponsible to try to meditate while the fire was still burning. Even though it was safely in the pit, what if an ember jumped out and set fire to the whole property?

We live in a desert!

It's the Californian war cry.

By the time the fire had almost burnt out and I'd dowsed it with water, the sun was setting. I couldn't put it off any longer.

Once more, I got myself settled, sitting cross-legged on the cushion, and... finally... I closed my eyes.

I willed myself not to open my eyes. I kept them closed and started to breathe deeply. I counted six in and eight out. Every time my mind tried to wander, I brought it back again. I breathed in and I breathed out. I did nothing but breathe. I banished everything and everyone from my mind. It was hard. Star came in a *lot*. No, not in *that* way, it was the words she'd said to me about deserving good things, about me needing to love myself more. I realized they were burning in me. I didn't know what to do with them.

I fought and fought, pushing it all away.

And finally there was peace.

Everything was quiet again. I knew I was awake. I just knew it. I was completely conscious – I had probably never been so conscious. But I couldn't hear anything, or feel anything. There was just nothing.

Until I heard the voice.

Say you love me.

WHAT?!

I felt really uncomfortable, like I wanted to run away but was paralysed. I knew I could get up and run away but I kind of couldn't at the same time. Nothing made any sense.

Say you love me.

What? No. Who are you?

I'm you. Say you love me.

Okaaaay…

A little awareness of my surroundings came back as I opened my mouth. I told myself to say the words.

"I…"

Nothing.

Fuck! What was wrong with me?

"I…"

The words were sticking in my throat. They weren't coming out. I began to panic; it was as if I'd lost control of my body.

"I… I… I…"

One last big effort.

"I HATE YOU! I FUCKING HATE YOU! YOU STUPID, STUPID PIECE OF SHIT! I HATE YOU!"

My eyes sprung open as the tears literally spurted out of my eyes and flooded down my cheeks. I was gasping and gulping down air as I wailed. This level of crying was like nothing I'd ever experienced in my life. The grief that was pouring out of me was a river of blackness. I held my hands over my chest as if I was holding in my heart that was in danger of falling out of my body.

"I hate you, so much," I said through my desperate tears. "I'm sorry, I'm sorry, but I do!"

And in that admission – and apology – there was a tiny shard of relief. Something I had been hiding from was out there in front of me. Obviously I didn't have a clue what to do with it in that moment but at least I had spoken its name.

HATE!

We weren't allowed to use the word "hate" when we were growing up. "I may not like you sometimes, but I'll always love you," my mother would tell us when we accused her of hating us for not letting us do something we wanted to do. "And 'hate' is a very strong word."

She wasn't kidding.

I had just felt the full strength of it.

"I don't like the look of it at all," said the King. "However, it may kiss my hand if it likes."

Alice's Adventures in Wonderland,
Chapter 8

LEWIS CARROLL

CHAPTER SEVEN

The Girl Who Hated Herself

*Loving a broken person is like trying
to fill a bucket with holes in it.
It doesn't matter how much water you
pour into it… none will stay in.*

The day after you've discovered you loathe yourself with a passion and depth you didn't know you possessed is probably not the best time to go apartment hunting.

My first appointment was a darling studio apartment a few minutes walk away, across Sunset, on Larissa Drive. The Canadian actress who lived there was subletting for three months while she did a TV show in Toronto. It was in the upstairs corner of a Spanish style apartment complex with a little communal yard available for the six units in the building. Everything about it was lovely. Everything about *her* was lovely. The location was perfect. The price was a steal. I was the first person to see it. She had six appointments after me.

So I took it, right?

Nope. I told her I'd think about it.

★

I picked up a coffee and a box of donuts (I needed to eat a *lot* of feelings) from the minimart in the strip mall on the corner of Lucile and made my way over to the far side of Los Feliz. What I refer to as the "near side" – as in near to Silver Lake – of Los Feliz is lovely. It's still got the Silver Lake vibe. But anywhere west of Vermont loses a little of that sparkle. There is row upon row of beige 1960s apartment blocks with an occasional smattering of neo-Gothic style, bordered by streets of large, imposing Craftsman style houses. It was up to one of these houses that I pulled up. The property was fenced off from the street behind high steel railings that were painted dark duck egg to match the house.

The woman who answered the door reminded me of Aunt Josephine, as played by Meryl Street in *A Series of Unfortunate Events*. She immediately came across as completely obsessive and neurotic. The house inside reflected her demeanour. It was crammed full of who knows what, things teetering on the edges of over-crowded shelves and bulging out of closets that couldn't be kept closed anymore. It was also a menagerie. I counted at least twenty living things, which included several human beings and about eight other species. There was a green parrot, a giant lizard that looked like a toy dinosaur, three aquariums filled with fish and sea snakes, and an aging British drummer who said he'd been in a very famous band in the 80s. I hadn't heard of it. He also said he was 50. He was 70 if he was a day. His hair was grey, his skin was grey, his teeth were grey… he looked like he was in stage make-up he was so grey (maybe he was). The available room to rent was in the basement where there was a lingering smell of damp clothes, lemon-scented cleaning fluid and cat litter (when it hasn't been changed for several weeks).

Could I live in a place like this in a million years?

I told her I'd think about it.

Next stop was a massive apartment block on the corner of Los Feliz and Griffith Park Boulevards. I went up to the third floor in the tiny elevator and emerged to find myself in a dimly lit, windowless corridor that was so long it disappeared into darkness. I edged my way down it – the walls seeming to close in on me, wondering how long I'd last in this place with my claustrophobia. The apartment had two bedrooms that were directly next to each other… and one bathroom. My roomies would be a couple who had just got married, and clearly wanted to ensure that no one forgot the fact. They sat in front of me stroking each other like you'd stroke a cat. I told them I might be interested in the place. They said they were making a shortlist and they'd let me know if I made the cut.

I left and made my way over to Atwater Village where I walked into a house full of semi-professional snowboarders and walked out high as a kite. That was how I learned that "420-friendly" did not refer to an obscure freeway I had never discovered, like the blissfully quiet 2 Freeway (and now everyone in Eagle Rock and Glendale hates me).

Back in Los Feliz and further up the hill, hanging off a cliff edge in the middle of the wilderness that fell away underneath the eastern edge of Griffith Park itself, I discovered a community of people who were looking for someone to "join" them; a woman, specifically. There were no designated bedrooms; the house was a free-for-all. You slept where – and with whom – you wanted when the moment took you. I didn't *smell* pot in here but there were some odd-looking eyeballs and facial tics, and a lot of grinning. And no one had noticed that the structure they were living in looked as though it was one small tremor away from breaking free and tumbling into the deep ravine. Luckily, my vertigo kicked in and I couldn't make it past the entrance way where they'd all gathered to inspect me.

I was excited to find a listing for one more apartment to rent in Silver Lake that was well within my budget. It was described as a "studio apartment with private entrance" and was actually an outside storage space adjoining the main house, which itself was infinitesimal; I'd seen bigger bathrooms. The owner was Scottish. She'd lived in the U.S. for 35 years without a green card, and was terribly proud of the fact, even though it meant she had never been able to leave, as she wouldn't have got back into the country, having overstayed her original visa by 33 years.

When I saw the locked doors to the store cupboard, I feared the worst, but that was nothing compared to the reality.

The landlady positioned a ladder that had been lying on the ground against the doors to the cupboard and invited me to climb up to see the space, which was *above* said store cupboard and accessed through a little hatch door. No joke. It was about seven by five feet, and a little over four feet high. It was *literally* a "crawl space". There was a mattress and a microwave. No natural light, unless you left the little hatch open. There was a large battery powered lantern on the floor.

"No candles" she warned me. No kidding!

When I enquired where I would charge my phone and laptop she frowned for a moment, like she hadn't considered this and considered her tenant's need for electric power an inconvenience.

"Well… I suppose you can use the sockets in the kitchen," she finally relented. "But I'll have to be charging you a little extra for the electricity."

However, included in the rent (she proudly announced) was access to the bathroom at any time of day or night, although I wasn't to turn on the main light after 10pm as it might wake her up since she liked to sleep with the bedroom door open. And "full kitchen privileges" were granted but times had to be agreed on in advance. Dishes could be washed at any time of day because we wouldn't want an infestation of cockroaches or rodents. *She expects me to eat my meals in this hole?*

She wanted $600 per month for the privilege of living in her "rental space" (she was honest enough not to call it a room). *You should be paying me $600 a month* was my only thought.

I didn't hate myself *quite* enough to take it.

There was a glimmer of light in the storm.

I had given myself a strict budget for rent. I was eking out my development fee for the TV pilot and if they didn't green light it soon, or I didn't sell another script (the New York feature film idea was stalling because my mojo was so low), I would be dipping into my modest pot of savings. I looked at rooms in houses in areas I'd never even heard of, like "Frogtown" and "Glassell Park" (home of one of the most notorious L.A. gangs, the landlord happily informed me.) I managed to say no to the truly outrageous or hideous. But invariably I said I'd consider somewhere only to be told, "Don't call us, we'll call you."

I called the Canadian actress. Obviously the guy who saw the place after me had paid a deposit on the spot. It had been the only good place I'd seen and I'd sabotaged my chances by not snapping it up.

And then I found the place, a place that perfectly reflected how I felt about myself at this point.

It was Silver Lake Adjacent, on a quiet street between the 5 Freeway and Ripple Street. Quiet in the sense that there was no traffic *on* the street. In terms of actual noise… the deep hum and muffled roar of freeway traffic passing barely 30 feet from your bedroom is a sound that stays with you forever. It was a two-storey building that looked as if it had been made out of paper and card. There were four units in the building and a room was available for rent in the downstairs unit, the one closest to the freeway.

My roommate was an odd fellow. He worked for UPS and his schedule never wavered by a minute. He got up at 7am, seven days a week. I'm not sure why he needed the alarm clock, which was set extra loud because of the freeway traffic noise; I would have thought his body clock was physically unable to wake up a minute either side of 7am. On weekdays he showered and left the house at 7.20am to go to work. On weekends he showered and left the house at 7.30am to go to the gym. I'm not sure what he did after the gym but he came home the same time on weekends as he did on weekdays, at exactly 6.30pm. He ate dinner in his room and watched movies until 11pm when he went to sleep.

His name was Patrick.

He'd clearly outlined his schedule to me when I viewed the place and the thought of having the space to myself for most of the day, every day, was so appealing, I overlooked the depressing surroundings.

The place was filthy. He'd lived there for eight years with his brother (whose room I was subletting) and I assume they had never properly cleaned it once. The one tiny bathroom between the bedrooms was covered in mould. The only redeeming feature about this place was Patrick's massive collection of books and DVDs. Literally one whole wall of the open plan living space had been turned into a library. Shelves from floor to ceiling seemed to contain every book, movie and TV show you could ever dream of owning. For someone with such low hygiene standards, Patrick had surprisingly good taste.

I moved in and spent an entire day cleaning the place before I set about browsing the vast DVD collection.

The first movie that caught my eye was one I'd heard good things about but had never seen.

The Soloist is a remarkable film with stunning performances from Robert Downey Jr. and Jamie Foxx. It dramatizes the true story of Nathaniel Ayers, a homeless man living on the streets just off Skid Row in Downtown Los Angeles, who was discovered and befriended by *L.A. Times* journalist, Steve Lopez. Lopez was inspired to investigate what had led to Ayers, a Juilliard-trained cellist, ending up on the streets. There is one scene – a particularly depressing scene – that takes place in a homeless shelter. Nathaniel Ayers is playing a section from the first Bach Cello Suite when his sister appears at the door. She has been estranged from him for years; she didn't even know if he was alive. She sits beside him, overcome with emotion. He doesn't acknowledge her for a while. Finally, he stops playing and glances at her – there's a moment of recognition and he says, "We had some life?"

141

I had to pause the movie because I couldn't stop crying. My future taunted me like a nightmare. I imagined myself in 30 years' time, a failed writer, penniless and homeless in L.A., dressed in stinking clothes, with greasy grey hair clinging to my neck in matted strands. I'm kneeling on the sidewalk, writing bad poetry with a small piece of chalk. I look up and there's my sister. She's found me after a 30-year search. She shakes her head in disbelief at what's become of me, tears rolling down her cheeks.

I stare up at her blankly, trying to place her.

I once lived just off Fairfax, across the road from the Farmers' Market. I regularly went to that Starbucks. There was a homeless woman who came in every day. She dragged behind her a suitcase held together with brown packing tape. She wore a filthy bathrobe – that had obviously once been white – over her clothes, and walked in cheap slippers that were barely staying on her feet. The stench of urine that hung around her was, unfortunately, so bad that the manager couldn't let her sit inside. She had a designated outside table, the one furthest from the door. We all bought her coffee and food. She never thanked us. She never looked at anyone, or spoke to anyone. She stared at the ground, as if in shame.

Like Lopez, I used to wonder what could happen to a person to lead them to end up like this. Perhaps one day, during an attempt to meditate, she'd discovered that she hated herself.

I lived on pasta for a couple of weeks. I didn't even feel like pesto. I boiled pasta and just stirred in some olive oil and salt and pepper. Sometimes I added ketchup. I watched three seasons of *24* but gave up in season four because it just gets silly. Some days I walked to Trader Joe's; it took 25 minutes. Often I bought more pasta and not much else. Mango sorbet would have melted before I got it home. I didn't take the car because I was maintaining the illusion that I still lived in Silver Lake, and walking distance from Trader Joe's. Sometimes it was the little lifeline I held onto.

Some days I cried; some days I didn't.

Anything could set me off.

I thought a hair cut was in order. I had been growing it for several years. The ex liked it long. It would be good to get some weight off my shoulders. Despite the fact that I'd sworn I'd never let anyone touch my locks but Emma, who'd been looking after my hair since we were 19 and she was a trainee at a fancy Kensington High Street salon, I booked an appointment at Fandango. I'd always wanted to go inside that blue Art Deco building on the corner of Griffith Park Boulevard.

I sat in the chair and asked a stranger to cut away my pain.

Forty minutes later, the sweet guy with a thousand piercings around his ears and nose showed me his creation from the front, back and sides.

I burst into tears and sobbed uncontrollably for a solid five minutes.

"I'm so sorry. It's not your fault," I told the traumatised kid. "It's really beautiful." I'm not sure that final word was ever completely formed within the wail that accompanied it.

I found every Pixar movie on Patrick's bookshelves and halfway through *Finding Nemo*, when Dory is repeating to herself, "Just keep swimming, just keep swimming, just keep swimming, swimming, swimming…" I yelled at the screen, "No! I don't want to swim anymore, just let me drown!"

And on came the waterworks again.

On the days I didn't make the trek over to Trader Joe's I made myself walk at least once around Silver Lake Reservoir.

One day I saw a Golden Retriever pushing the body of a dead mouse with his nose, as if willing it to move and play with him.

"It's dead!" I snapped at the poor dog, as I walked by. "It's *never* coming back to life."

The sudden realization about what I needed to do stopped me in my tracks.

I even forgot to cry.

I'd been carrying around with me, for more than a year, a bag of the ex's things. Little things I'd kept with me, for comfort, whenever we were apart for a stretch of time. There was an old rugby shirt of his that I used to sleep in, a beautiful card he'd written to me in an out-of-character poetic moment, a book that he'd given me. A pair of his socks (huge, knee-length sports socks) balled up – I would sometimes sleep with them when I missed him too much. The menu from the time we got upgraded to Upper Class on Virgin Atlantic flying from London to New York and *nearly* joined the mile-high club before I chickened out because I convinced myself they would have installed secret security cameras inside the smoke alarms in the toilets.

And a few other odds and ends.

I bagged up the clothing and books to take to Goodwill.

Then I took the card and the menu and any other bits of useless paper I'd been hoarding to a responsible spot on the driveway and burnt them in an empty tin can.

I said goodbye to him, properly, in my heart, forever.

A year after it was over, it was finally over.

I didn't feel better after this "letting go" ritual; if anything, I felt worse. In fact, I had never felt so empty in my life. I couldn't write a thing. There was nothing left inside me. I stopped going on stupid dates with myself. I wasn't even writing my journal documenting my story anymore. What was the point? What was there to say about being a Darcyless Bridget Jones? Or Elizabeth Gilbert without a travel budget? I'd eaten too much, forgotten to pray, and mistaken lust for love.

It felt like I was on punishment. I was in that period when you can't bring yourself to break up with someone so you just start treating them *really* badly hoping they'll do it first.

I'd figured something out, though. Dating yourself is like an arranged marriage. You didn't choose it and you can't get out of it. Well, except for the worst possible way. And I wasn't there yet. (With hindsight, I was probably closer than I realized but not, thankfully, quite there.)

I got thrown a timely lifeline by Natalie, who called me one Saturday desperate for a babysitter.

Natalie was another acquisition from Molly. She had once been a waitress for Molly but after her boyfriend left her, six months pregnant and in debt, she managed to put herself through law school and was now working as a paralegal for a big criminal defense attorney Downtown.

She'd rented an apartment two blocks from her office for herself and Stella, the little firecracker that had been worth every second of the shit her dumb ex had put her through.

So I'd known Stella since she was a baby. Being a big fan of babies and kids myself, I was always happy to fill in and save Natalie some dollars in babysitters when I could.

On this particular occasion, she'd booked a babysitter because she had a hot date, but the girl had let her down an hour before Natalie was due to leave.

"I'm so sorry, Jess, I know it's Saturday night and you probably have plans," she said over the phone, making me realize how long it had been since we'd caught up. "I shouldn't really ask you, it's only a date, but he's *great*. Seriously. Works in the DA's office. First nice guy I've met in… honestly… probably since I left North Carolina."

I grabbed my keys.

"Already in the car," I told her. "Put your lipstick on."

Hanging out with Stella was my idea of heaven and I knew she'd make me feel heaps better. She was exceptionally smart and funny. She had taken her status as the child of a single parent with a pinch of salt. Although Natalie swears she never said one bad word again Stella's dad (he had her every other Sunday, no overnights yet), when Stella was only five, her dad dropped her home one day, and she walks in and rolls her eyes at Stella and says, "That guy is *such* a schmuck, what were you thinking?" Then she crawls onto Stella's lap, gives her a massive hug and says, "Oh, yeah, that's right, about getting *me*!"

While Natalie went for sushi with her future husband (literally, I never let them forget the fact that I facilitated their first date), Stella and I had our own date. We ordered pizza and watched episodes of her favourite TV show, *Oswald*. It was really aimed at a slightly younger audience, but we'd watched it together since she was two years old. It was our thing. It's an animated series, narrated in the most soothing voice, about a blue octopus called Oswald, a penguin called Henry, and a daisy called… Daisy.

I stole a glass of champagne from Natalie's precious stock.

Natalie had been a heavy drinker once. She stopped for two years a few years before having Stella and went to AA; did the whole programme. But abstaining completely made her too miserable. So once she felt she'd "done the work" she set up some rules for herself.

She was allowed one glass of champagne every day. She kept the glass in the door of the refrigerator and took tiny sips throughout the day. Obviously she didn't drink any of it when she was at work but she never had drunk at work so that wasn't hard for her. She stretched out the one glass until there was one last sip left, which she took just before bed, knowing that there was another one to start in the morning. She wasn't allowed to drink outside her own home, even if she had to travel for several days. They were very, very strict rules. Of course she couldn't very well go back to AA and stand up every time saying, "Hello, I'm Natalie, I'm an alcoholic and I last had a drink when I took my hourly sip of champagne at five o'clock," but she kept in touch with the friends she'd made there, and batted away their accusations that she was in denial about her ongoing problem. She promised them that if she *ever* broke one of *her* rules – poured even one more sip of champagne out of the bottle in one 24-hour period, or drank on vacation, for example – she would come back to a meeting and get completely sober again. Some of them – possibly quite correctly – told her she wasn't a true alcoholic because if she was, she wouldn't have been able to control her drinking like that.

At bedtime I told Stella she could have as many stories as she liked. She requested five.

As we came to the end of *Big Red Barn*, the one I liked to finish with because all the animals go to bed at the end of it, indicating that it was time for *everybody* to go to bed, Stella looked up at me and, with the negotiating power that was clearly in her genes, said, "If I can have just *one more* story I totally promise I will go *straight* to sleep."

I already knew what she'd choose. We hadn't had our absolute favourite book yet. I knew she'd been saving it for this pre-planned encore.

I opened the book and we started reading together.

We had read it so many times she knew all the words. We started together.

"In the great green room, there was a telephone, and a red balloon, and a picture of—"

"The cow jumping over the moon!" Stella said, before I could even turn the page.

As we read on, I could feel myself hesitating, lingering over the pages. Something was coming I suddenly didn't want to hear.

We said goodnight to the room, and the moon, and the cow, and the light and the red balloon, and the bears and chairs and kittens and mittens and socks and clocks... and we got up to the comb, and then the brush, and then... I paused before turning the page and I could feel Stella's eyes on me.

"Goodnight nobody," she said, still looking at me.

I turned two pages in quick succession and said, "Goodnight mush," but it stuck in my throat a bit, and Stella didn't join in.

"Jessica, why are you crying," she asked me.

"I'm not," I lied. "I have a little cold."

"No you don't."

"It's the gluten from the pizza. Now say good night to the old lady whispering hush."

"You look sad," Stella said, taking my hand in hers, which obviously set me off completely. "It's okay. I don't mind you being sad. Me and Mom get sad loads of times. You just have to wait a while and then you feel happy again. You can't be happy all the time. But when you feel sad, you've got to remember that you *will* feel happy again. That's just what happens."

I hugged her tightly. There was nothing more to say.

We said goodnight to the stars and the air and the noises everywhere, I gave her one more hug, tucked her in and went to leave the room. I got to the door and she said, "Jessica."

I turned around. Here we go, I thought, the negotiating to stay up longer, even come and watch TV with me because she wasn't tired. But she floored me.

"Do you think maybe you need just *one more* hug?"

I couldn't speak. I just nodded and went back to her bed and curled up beside her.

And that's where Natalie found me when she tiptoed in at 2am.

While I was still, to all intents and purposes, a "bowl full of mush", I'd at least had my heart temporarily reheated by the love of a beautiful child.

And it's probably this that made it possible for me to even notice the sign on the little wooden building on Rowena that said, "THIS SATURDAY: Join us for a day of healing! FREE classes. Yoga. Sound baths. Reiki Healing."

Well, I thought to myself, there's no doubt, no doubt in the world, that I could use a little healing in my life.

I showed up early at the little healing centre and when it all kicked off, I got straight into one of the sound baths. It was glorious, lying on these huge cushions while some dude stirred imaginary porridge in a variety of metal bowls, creating the most extraordinarily sweet cacophony of sounds.

Next I had a tarot card reading.

I picked the death card (of course) but the woman with the huge purple turban on her head told me this was a great card because it meant the necessary ending of something and a wonderful new beginning. I also picked cards that told me I was going to meet the love of my life… the *real* one; my soulmate.

My heart leapt but I quickly shoved it down again. I didn't need any false promises right now; I just wanted to feel better.

I was excited when it was my turn to visit the Reiki healer in her little den. I had heard about this Reiki malarkey and had always wanted to try it. But it's hard to spend money on something if you've absolutely no idea what goes on. I soon discovered… not very much.

The smiley curvy woman told me to lie on my back on a table. Then she waved her hands over me for a while. Finally, she stood behind my head for a bit, and then went back to waving her hands over my legs.

"Hmm," she said. "You have a very playful spirit."

"Really," I said. "Well tell him I haven't been laughing much of late. Please try harder."

She laughed; and then stopped abruptly.

"Oh, your legs are not happy," she said sombrely.

Huh?

"You have very, very sad legs. They are very unhappy, your legs."

Well, yeah, I'd be clinically depressed if I was a leg attached to my body at the moment.

"You need to make friends with your legs."

Now it was my turn to laugh.

"I'm sorry," I said. "Make *friends* with my legs?"

"Yes," she said gently, placing her hands on her hips as if giving me a cue to leave. "There's a yoga class starting in a few minutes. I think you should go."

It was years since I'd done yoga, and for some strange reason I found myself filled with trepidation. And it wasn't about what had happened to me in the past (I'd once put my lower back out really badly doing yoga, which had led to the diagnosis of hypermobility and a long recovery period) or what the Reiki woman had just said. It was the death card in the Tarot reading. As I walked into the class, I had this feeling that something was about to change completely.

I probably held back a bit. Physically because of the old war wound, my back; emotionally because something in me was tightly wound up and damn well wanted to stay that way.

I eased myself in slowly. The teacher had said it was only a 20-minute taster class but I wasn't taking too many chances.

Some sun salutations were followed by some standing poses, and then we did some seated stretching.

"Seated eagle pose," said the majestic German yoga teacher with zero body fat or hair.

I copied my fellow yogis and sat on a block, one leg twisted right across and on top of the other. I stretched out my arms, crossed one over the other, palms together, as instructed, and stretched them up.

And that's when it happened.

Imagine one of those reclosable plastic storage bags that's closed tight shut. And then think of that feeling when you pull it apart, when you take either side of the plastic and pull it open.

That's what I felt happen in my back.

It was, literally, the opening of the floodgates.

This wasn't like the crying I'd done on the treehouse terrace, it wasn't like the crying I'd done during *The Soloist*, or *Finding Nemo*. It wasn't like the crying in Fandango or over *Goodnight Moon*. This was just like I'd opened a bag and water came spilling out. Tears just flooded, actually flooded down my cheeks. There was no gasping, no gulping, no heaving, no noise.

Just tears.

Nothing more.

No drama.

Just me.

In a Pool of Tears.

I got up slowly, grabbed my bag and crept out of the yoga class. I headed to the bathroom. I locked the door and sank to the floor, shrinking into the corner under the washbasin.

152

The tears were still streaming down my face and body. I chugged as much as I could from my water bottle for fear of dehydration.

I wasn't aware of time passing but at some point I realized that the tears had stopped. I felt very tired. Very, very tired. I managed to haul myself up into a standing position and looked at my reflection in the mirror above the washbasin.

It was like seeing myself for the first time. I studied myself, with curiosity.

The skin on my face, stretched over those Slavic cheekbones, was blotchy from all the crying, but still fairly flawless. My eyes were bright, bright green, as they always were when I was emotional. Or drunk (thus also emotional). I'd always hated my nose. I looked at it now. It was too big, but at least it was straight and hadn't been bent and made crooked in a rough rugby tackle like *some* people's.

I touched the little scar just under my chin from when I'd split it open by diving into the shallow end of a swimming pool years ago. And then lowered my hand to my neck. In this light I couldn't see the scar where my mother had held me by my throat as she submerged my entire body into cold water after I'd poured a pan of boiling water over myself when I was two years old. I ran my hand through my ultra fine – though plentiful – dark blonde hair, still unused to where it finished just below my ear. I looked at the little gap in my left eyebrow where I'd got a little pluck-happy with a pair of tweezers a few years before, where the hair had never grown back. I studied the little gaps in pigment in my top lip, which made them look so different when I covered them in lipstick, which I didn't do often.

Impulsively I reached out and touched my reflection.

"I'm sorry," I whispered. "I'm really sorry. I will try harder. I'm sorry."

And then I looked down at the lower half of my 5'6" frame and gently touched my big, chunky thighs.

"I'm saying sorry to you, too," I said to them. "I guess we're in this together."

I looked up at my reflection again. I knew what it was like to try and love a broken person. I'd dated so many of them. I was a seeker and collector of broken souls. I could detect them from miles away. And look what I'd gone and done. I'd picked another one. Oh, I was broken for sure.

I knew all too well that loving a broken person is like trying to fill a bucket with holes in it. It doesn't matter how much water you pour into it... none will stay in.

I was a bucket full of holes.

I was looking at a broken woman.

The question was... could I fix her?

If you drink much from a bottle marked 'poison,' it is almost certain to disagree with you, sooner or later.

Alice's Adventures in Wonderland,
Chapter 4

LEWIS CARROLL

CHAPTER EIGHT

The Girl Who Figured Some Things Out

Our scars make us what we are.

What had gone so horribly, horribly wrong that I ended up thirty-something, single and weeping on the floor of a yoga studio in an eastern suburb of Los Angeles? I'd worked so hard to find the answers. I'd done the therapy, I'd read the books and said the mantras. Why hadn't it worked?

My first long-term relationship had ended during my first incarnation in L.A., but that time I'd been the heart-breaker. We were young; far too young to be doing a long-distance relationship. I thought I was in love, but after long discussions with my friends, I accepted that I wasn't actually *in love* with him; I was just in love with the fact that he loved *me* so much. Well, he never really stood a chance with me because he was a *whole* person, and – as we later discovered – I only knew how to love *broken* souls.

I couldn't shake the guilt of breaking his heart and I had a few sessions of therapy, which were interesting. I got some "tools" and did a little digging around but probably only managed a few temporary patch-ups. The real damage was so deeply buried I'd need an industrial excavator to have any chance of reaching it.

The therapy precipitated a journey of self-discovery… of sorts. I read all the right books. I followed Deepak Chopra's "spiritual laws", found my "peaceful warrior" with Dan Millman, "healed my body" with Louise Hay, found my "vein of gold" with Julia Cameron. I'd felt the fear, did it anyway, made the "four agreements", travelled my heart and mind with *The Alchemist* and *The Little Prince*, walked the "less travelled" road and reached my "tipping point".

I'd written letters to my former and future selves.

"I love you," I'd written a thousand times. But that was all before I discovered that the true test was to *say* it. I'd failed that test because I didn't know that the love I'd been trying to give myself was leaking out as fast as I tried to pour it in because… *you can't fill a bucket full of holes.*

Over the years, I had tried a bit more therapy, but nothing stuck. Finding a good therapist – someone who is right for *you* – is like searching for a needle in a haystack and, seriously, who has the time?

In my trawl through the self-help shelves, I discovered Geneen Roth. When I saw the title of her book, *When You Eat at the Refrigerator, Pull Up a Chair*, I let out a little yelp of joy and recognition in the middle of Skylight Books. But while her words resonated deeply, nothing *changed* in me. I heard someone speak about the difference between "knowing, doing and being." You can *know* something, but until you start *doing* it, nothing will change. And the real transformation happens when you don't even have to consciously do it anymore, you're just automatically "being" it. But where did I start?

Well I'd been given some new insight by the Reiki woman;

apparently my thighs were very unhappy. So maybe that was a place to start.

I was born fat. In other words, I was born healthy. I weighed a modest, but healthy, 7lb 2oz and emerged into this world with a head covered in tight black curls, that later turned into blonde wisps. I elongated rapidly and by the time I started school, was the one of the tallest girls in my class. The fat got stretched out, so I became a skinny kid… and a super bendy one. I could touch my toes – going forwards *and* backwards – and do the splits both ways.

First I wanted to be an ice skater, then I wanted to be a ballerina, then I wanted to be a gymnast. I didn't like team sports; I wasn't particularly competitive and my reflexes weren't top notch so I'd generally end up letting the side down. Anyway, none of this was remotely relevant because the only thing that interested my mother was my academic grades. She came from a generation and family where formal education was your passage to a better life and naturally pushed me to do well. Sending me to a frightfully upper class British boarding school, when we had neither the breeding nor the budget to keep up with the Joneses (or rather the *Pettifer*-Joneses) was perhaps a push too far.

From day one, I felt ashamed: ashamed that I didn't have the correct name, ashamed that I didn't live in the right part of the country, ashamed that I was always crying because I was so homesick, and ashamed that I regularly wet my bed (probably on account of all of the above). Matron, during those early years, was a rotund witch with greasy grey hair that fell almost to her waist (she normally kept it in a bun but I'd seen her in the middle of the night and was able to confirm its full length). She chain-smoked. When you had to knock on her door in the middle of the night – crying, with wet pyjamas – you half choked to death when she opened it. You would cough and splutter, blinking in the bright light of her bedroom, watching those shrivelled hands with their long yellow talons for fingernails, come into view through the clouds of smoke.

I was skinny until I was 13. Then puberty arrived and within one week I had sprouted breasts and my thighs had doubled in size. I couldn't wear my pointe shoes any more because my balance was all off while I readjusted to a new centre of gravity, so I gave up ballet. I got worse at team sports because I got even slower. I was still good at swimming – I'd always had good form and strength in the water – and usually did well in competitions, but at my school, no one was interested in individual achievements, it was all about the team. So you weren't as cool when you were a swimmer, or track athlete, as you were if you were good at netball and lacrosse.

I hated being fat. Fat was highly unfashionable at my school. The girls reminded me of the importance of being thin every day. They would snatch away my plate of toast at breakfast, or steal my puddings at lunch because, they said, "Aren't you on a diet?" and when I complained, they'd say, "We're just trying to help you. You'd be so pretty if you lost weight." They were past masters at the backhanded compliment. Another was, "You look like Madonna. We don't think she's pretty but lots of people do."

I've looked back at photos of this period. They all look like Twiggy (circa. 1967); I look normal. I was not as fat as I thought.

★

Amber was kind to me, even though she was considered (by the girls who mattered) a cut above me, on account of her super skinny body. They decreed her out of my league but she stuck by me all the way through school. We could never be *official* best friends, but in private she always reassured me that I was her *real* best friend. When we compared bodies, I would hanker after her skinny legs, while she envied my boobs, her own chest being virtually as flat as a pancake. She had two almost imperceptible anthills where her breasts should have been, that you'd hardly notice, even under the tightest of t-shirts.

These discussions obviously marked our rite of passage into womanhood, teaching us that we would *always*, for the rest of our lives, hanker after anyone else's attributes whilst despising our own assets.

On my 14th birthday I got caught smoking with Amber and Allegra (her official best friend). I confessed to having brought the cigarettes into school so they got warnings and I got suspended for a week.

My mother was furious. She stood in our kitchen and lectured me at the top of her voice for over an hour while I watched, nervously, as she smoked three cigarettes, working out that there were two left in the pack and wondering how long it would be until I could steal one.

The more I tried to diet, the more my thighs grew... because I yo-yo dieted: starving myself for a week and then falling off the wagon and eating everything in sight for two days straight.

My right thigh also grew at an alarming rate one day,

doubling in size within an hour. But there was a specific reason for that.

The February after the smoking incident, we had a sudden cold snap and the whole country got covered in a massive blanket of snow.

Outside our boarding house was a grass bank that sloped down to the tennis courts. It wasn't particularly long or steep and the ground flattened out for about ten feet before you reached the tall, steel posts that held up the wire mesh fencing around the tennis courts.

This was a perfect little hill to sledge down.

On tin trays.

Everyone took it in turns to use the slightly battered tin trays we sneaked out of the kitchens to slide down the snowy slope. You'd get a fair speed up and stop a couple of feet from the tennis court fencing.

I'd been home for the weekend and had brought back and smuggled in (assuring my father it was allowed and then somehow hiding it in the boot room) my super fast wooden sled because there were some big hills on the other side of the woods and on Saturdays we were allowed to go off there.

I was keen to win popularity points and I knew this sled was impressive, so I decided to use it instead of the tin trays on the grass bank.

I brought my sled to the top of the little slope and sat on it. I pushed myself off and went speeding down the hill to a chorus of cheers. The thrill of being the source of such entertainment, the sound of the applause, the experience of being centre of attention, filled me with delight, momentarily. But in the next moment I was in a panic. Why wasn't the sled stopping at the bottom of the hill? (Damn me for not paying more attention to the effects of friction on speed in physics!) I was actually accelerating towards the metal post holding up the fencing around the tennis court.

Realizing I had better jump ship, fast, before I crashed headlong, and at speed, into this solid metal post, I swung my left leg to one side in an attempt to dismount… but alas, not in time. I slammed right into the post. Well, my inner thigh did!

And then I experienced being the centre of attention and the source of great entertainment for a whole week.

But not in a nice way.

My inner thigh doubled in size with the swelling. Partly because matron (by now a sadist who would turn off the hot water as punishment and make us take cold showers) was so angry with me for smuggling in my fancy sled without permission, she refused to take me to the hospital. Or even give me an ice pack. So I waddled around in agonizing pain, legs astride to avoid putting any pressure on that tender, multi-coloured, watermelon-sized bruise.

"You look like a duck trying to give birth!"

"You look like your tampon's got stuck halfway out!"

As if my thighs hadn't had enough abuse for a lifetime, they once became the source of ridicule for a whole weekend. This time it was the boys who took all the shots.

We were taking the train to Yorkshire. Harriet Willoughby-Smith had invited 12 people to her 16th birthday party at her family's stately home near Castle Howard. Amber had begged her to invite me. It was the first week of the Christmas holidays. My October birthday always made me the youngest in my year. Technically I was in a year above the one I should have been in. (My whole life I wondered if I would have had a different experience at school if I'd stayed in the right year. The girls in the year below me definitely *seemed* less bitchy than those in my year, and the years above me were increasingly *more* bitchy, so perhaps bitchiness got diluted down the generations.) Allegra was a whole year and two weeks older than me. Amber's birthday was at the end of June so she was only a little older than me.

We all met at King's Cross Station to get the train to York. There were four boys joining us for the journey: one from Eton and three from Radley. The two other boys who were invited lived in Yorkshire and would join us there; they were at Ampleforth. I looked forward to seeing one of them, Marcus. When we were really drunk at a party in London the previous summer, he'd confessed to me that he'd been made to report to the prefect's study, for answering back, where he was forced to give four older boys blowjobs. The next day he made me promise never to tell, and it had made me feel like we had a special bond, that I had an ally. But I was dreading the journey with the others, particularly Rupert and Hugo. Piers, from Eton, who was going out with Allegra, was quiet, and the other boy from Radley was going through a "goth" phase and had gone all moody and sulky but posed no real threat, but Rupert and Hugo were loud, obnoxious and – when we found them pushing each other around on luggage trollies on the main concourse – clearly already drunk, despite it being only 9am.

"Yesssss! It's thunder thighs!" Rupert greeted me as we all rocked up. Hugo howled with laughter. Amber scolded them and ushered them both – as they started weaving around imaginary slalom poles – onto the train.

It was relentless, the whole journey. They never let up.

"Do you need two seats, TT? One for each thigh!"

"What are you feeding the other one?" Pointing to my right leg as I ate a sandwich from the snack bar.

"Can't find the bottle opener. Put that between your legs and crack it open, there's a darling!" said Hugo, handing me an unopened bottle of beer. "But don't drink it. Think of the calories!"

"A moment on the lips; a lifetime on the hips!" Rupert falsetto-ed.

We arrived at the castle (not *actually* Howard, but not far off in size I imagine) and were shown to our bedrooms by various chambermaids, having been told to dress for dinner and meet in the library in an hour for drinks.

I got lost, in the east wing, and was the last to arrive in the library.

"Now, everyone be kind to Thunder Thighs and keep her away from the salmon blinis," Rupert said loudly, grabbing a plate off a table and holding it up in the air so I couldn't reach it.

"Rupert! Stop it!" Amber admonished him. But the fact that she had to protect me just added to my embarrassment.

Much, much later, after I'd been assured that biting on some shot that had been left in the pheasant was "frightfully lucky" despite the fact that I was sure it had chipped my tooth, we were congregated in the red drawing room. The boys were playing pool on the full-sized snooker table.

Or some mad version of it where you had to drink a different sized shot of rum depending on the colour of the ball you potted.

Sir Thomas Willoughby-Smith ("call me Tom") came to sit beside me on the sofa.

"Are you okay, darling? I hear the boys are being rather beastly to you," he said, gently patting one of the thunder thighs. Harriet was the youngest of four so her father was older than most of our fathers. He was probably getting close to 60. Excessive drinking had caused his face to become a mass of broken veins and he had very little hair left on his head, but you could tell he had once been a very handsome man. Harriet's mother was the second Lady Willoughby-Smith and had been nanny to the two children birthed by the *first* Lady Willoughby-Smith.

"I'm okay," I reassured him, with a weak smile.

"Look, if you ask me, it's all a ruse. The buggers probably fancy the pants off you but they can't admit it in case you turn them down. So they're happy getting attention by stirring you up. Just ignore them."

I actually laughed out loud. It was the first time I'd laughed all day and it felt good.

"That's funny!" I said. But he raised his eyebrows at me.

"Trust me, I know a thing or two about young blokes, and they're only horrid like that to girls they want to roger."

Around 2am, when the third bottle of 20-year-old single malt was being opened and every piece of furniture had been danced on, I slipped off to go to the loo, after getting explicit instructions from the old man, who had stuck by my side, which meant the boys had left me alone.

On my way back, down a long, dark corridor, I saw Sir Tom coming towards me. He was holding onto the walls; he'd probably drunk around half of the total whiskey that had been consumed that night.

"Did you find the loo, darling?"

"Yes, thank you," I said, suddenly desperately hoping I was going to be able to slip past him and carry on back to the drawing room. Something suddenly made me feel uncomfortable. But he got in front of me – just-turned-15-year-old me – and grabbed hold of my arms.

"Now, you're to remember what I said, okay," he said.

"Yes," I assured him, gently trying to pull away. But he tightened his grip on my arms.

"You're not to be upset. They're just teasing because you're so bloody gorgeous." He pulled me towards him, and despite the champagne and the wine and the Scotch and whatever else we'd been served to drink, I suddenly felt completely sober. And scared. "You are, you know… bloody gorgeous. Sexy little filly, you are," he slurred. The alcohol fumes emerging from his mouth hit me and made me cough. As I did, he put a hand on my left breast and planted a sloppy, whisky-and-cigar flavoured kiss on my lips.

Like a lithe cat, I squirmed out of his grasp and took a couple of steps backwards, staring at him in shock.

"Oh, don't look at me like that," he snarled. His mood changed like the wind. "I was only feeling sorry for you. Thought it might cheer you up a bit to get a kiss. Nothing in it."

I turned and marched back to the drawing room. Where I drank Scotch until I passed out. I woke up in bed with Marcus.

167

We couldn't remember how we'd got there, but we were fully clothed.

It could have been so much worse.

But Sir Tom was right about one thing.

Several years later, Amber invited me on a group holiday to Portugal. It was the summer after we all graduated from university. I'd gone to London, to get away from everyone, who variously went to Oxford, Cambridge, Bristol, Durham and Exeter. We hadn't kept in touch during our uni years, but as the 21st birthday parties started cropping up on the calendar (being held anywhere from Annabel's to Belize), I started to get a few invitations. I turned most of them down but I hesitated over Amber's. Her father had rented her a house on the Algarve.

She called me after I didn't write back immediately and asked me if I was coming. I asked who else was going. When she told me, I was even more hesitant. She begged me. I said I couldn't afford it. She offered to pay for my flights. I said I would have to see if I could get time off from my waitressing job.

I could get time off from my waitressing job, but only to join them two days into the trip. When I arrived on the Sunday, they'd been there (drinking solidly) since Friday.

I had been prepping myself all week for how to deal with Rupert and Hugo, but fortunately Hugo wasn't there; he'd got glandular fever a few days before the trip. Sadly, Marcus hadn't been invited. The boys (and so the girls) had kind of abandoned him when he'd come out at 19. I met him for a coffee in Soho once. "It turns out sucking dick is highly addictive," he'd told me. "Maybe more than smoking." But he seemed happier than I'd ever seen him so it was clearly *better* for you than smoking – a notion I lodged somewhere in the recesses of my mind.

I was thrown by the fact that Rupert, who looked pretty worse for wear after three days of solid drinking, didn't tease me. He didn't hurl any unkind words at me. He didn't hurl any words at me at all. He never even made eye contact. Maybe he lost his bravado without his sidekick, Hugo, around.

I didn't care. Him ignoring me suited me perfectly.

There was a lot of drinking and eating and dancing and taxis, and the bill was always split between the group no matter who had eaten or drunk what.

To ensure I could afford to go out on the very last night, I feigned a headache on the penultimate night (when a minibus was being hired to take everyone to a restaurant in a neighbouring town).

I stayed in my room, curled up on my bed in a t-shirt and leggings, and listened to the racket downstairs as they finished their pre-dinner drinks and piled into the minibus, all arguing about who would sit where and which club they'd go to after. I waited until the minibus had driven off before I emerged into the brightly lit house that smelled like the perfume counter at Harrods mingled with the pungent aromas of a brewery.

I went down to the kitchen, turning lights off in various rooms as I went, and opened the door of the refrigerator. I stood there and stared at the offerings – mostly little boxes of left-over food from picnic lunches and doggy bags from evening meals.

"Well, some things don't change." I jumped. And then

spun around to see Rupert standing in the doorway to the kitchen. "Except your thighs, which are bigger than ever." I immediately felt my cheeks burn and my palms go sweaty, but I was older and wiser now. I was 20, for fuck's sake, I had a degree; surely I could handle this.

"Look, Rupert, I think—"

"You know some of the boys are not happy." He was walking towards me. I closed the fridge door and edged around the counter away from him. "They're on *holiday*. Your fat bum squeezed into a bikini is not exactly what they've come to look at."

He was really close to me now. I'd actually never been this close to him. He was horribly good-looking, despite the effects of the alcohol on his skin. I'd never noticed before. He had these piercing green eyes, the same colour as mine. I felt a mix of attraction and revulsion as I clocked this.

"So if you wouldn't mind staying covered up tomorrow, I know the boys would appreciate it." He was really close to me. Because I'd never been this close to him, I had never realized how tall he was, probably close to 6'2" and I was only 5'6". I had no idea how to respond to his cruel words and I was scared, but also felt a flutter of pleasure because this good-looking, popular boy was paying me some attention. I immediately hated myself for that.

Now he was right in front of me. He took a few steps forward so that his body was pressing against mine and I could feel he was rock hard inside his jeans. He stood astride so that his head was more level with mine and pushed against me harder with his body. The edge of the kitchen counter dug into my back painfully.

"It's pretty simple. Some girls should wear bikinis and

some shouldn't," he murmured as he stuck his hand down my leggings and shoved two fingers inside me. It hurt like hell. But then he kissed me and it was a good kiss. I hated that he was one of the best kissers I had ever had and for a moment I got carried away and joined in, as if I'd spun into a parallel universe where being kissed by Rupert was an every-day and acceptable occurrence.

The confusing combination of pain and pleasure was too much for me and I burst into tears.

"Shit!" he spat. "I'm not sleeping with a cry baby." He grabbed me by the arms and looked at me, his eyes full of hatred and disgust and frustration… not good-looking any more at all.

"Listen," he hissed at me, ominously. "If you tell anyone, I'll deny it. They'd never believe you, anyway, everyone knows I hate you." He turned and stormed out of the kitchen… and probably into the shower to sort himself out.

I ran back up to my bedroom.

At least I was still a virgin.

There were many, many times I could have had sex before I turned 21. But I avoided them all, either by choice or luck.

When I was 18, I got my first job in a pub. I had a crush on the landlord, Steven. His wife was heavily pregnant, so he was a safe guy to have a crush on because nothing could ever happen, which is why I told one of the other bar staff (in total confidence) about my crush. Steven walked me home every night (to be safe), down the dark path that led to the wooden door in the back wall of our garden.

Two nights after I told my colleague (in confidence) about my crush, when it came to walking me home, Steven didn't bring the dog. I remember thinking this was strange. He always brought the dog. Why wouldn't you bring the dog on a short walk through the neighbourhood at midnight?

When we got to my garden door, Steven pushed me against it, covering my mouth with his and trying to force his tongue between my clamped shut lips.

Fortunately it was a hot summer's night and my mother (who habitually fell asleep on the couch after dinner until about 11pm and then got up and got on with various chores) was outside watering the garden.

"Jessica? Is that you?" she called out. Steven released me immediately.

That was a lucky escape.

Then there was lovely Andy. We'd become an item on a camping trip when I was 19. I'd been invited by a girl I knew at uni; the others were friends of hers from home. There was one couple (this girl from uni and her boyfriend), me, another bloke, and Andy. I had my pick of the two single blokes… I picked Andy.

We did lots of kissing and snuggling in our respective sleeping bags beside the campfire, but we were all in one big tent so no one was getting laid much. It would have been a bit rude.

We all went back to uni (me and Andy still officially an item) and I went up to see him in Edinburgh twice. I loved his housemates. I loved Edinburgh. And I was really, *really* fond of Andy. And *almost* sure I wanted to lose my virginity to him.

"Next time, definitely," I told him, as we kissed goodbye at Waverly Station the second time I visited. We'd *really* nearly done it that time, we got very… very close.

But there was no next time. Because the following week he called to break up with me. Officially.

He was officially the one that got away. I always called him that. He went on to marry an equally lovely girl and produce a brace of exceptionally lovely children.

"I wasn't good enough for him," I thought for many years, until I realized that we just weren't meant for each other.

This was a pattern, what had happened with Andy. It went on for a few years. I'd meet a boy, there would be a lot of kissing, we would be deemed boyfriend and girlfriend by default, I would get naked with him a couple of times but stop short of full penetrative sex saying, I just *wanted to be sure*. And he would break up with me just as I was on the verge of "being sure"... perhaps unable to deal with the frustration. Sex is what teenage boys want. Sex. Not kissing. Not a relationship. *Sex.* Everything is a route to SEX. But it's an obstacle course. If the wall gets too high to climb, they will try another one.

Or maybe it was just me.

Huw, an interesting guy I met doing that waitressing job, told me I was "a conquest not a catch," that I was the type of girl men didn't want to *be* with, they just wanted to have *had*. He was the Welsh chef. Happily married. He was excessively proclamatory. "Let me tell you something about men and women," he'd started with, before getting specific about me. "You see, here's the thing. Man goes out at night *hoping* to get lucky. Woman goes out at night *knowing* she'll get lucky. See. You hold *all* the cards, my love. *All* the cards." That bit was very interesting. Although it didn't exactly apply to me... someone who was paralysed by buried trauma but didn't know it.

Cards I may have held, but play them I knew not how.

Except one time... with the guy I did, finally, lose my virginity to.

I did believe, with all my heart, when I met Jake – a month before I turned 22 – that he was the love of my life and I'd be with him forever.

Or maybe I was just getting desperate to have my cherry popped.

Or maybe my need to find a broken soul to love kicked into overdrive.

Jake was a recovering heroin addict. This was *serious*. I had never, ever in my life met someone who had taken heroin, let alone someone who had become an addict, let alone someone who had become an *ex*-addict!

I should have walked away as soon as I found out, but my radar had spotted a bucket with a *lot* of holes and the little gauge was peaking, almost swinging off the scale.

I was living in a pretty cushy spot at the time. The week after I returned from Portugal, Amber had called me with a nice offer. (I never knew if it had anything to do with the episode with Rupert, or if she even knew about that, but something told me she *sensed* something pretty awful had happened, because I was a mess for the rest of the trip and she knew Rupert had stayed behind that night; she must have guessed *something* was amiss.)

Amber's grandmother had died, leaving a lovely one-bedroom flat in Notting Hill. Probate was going to be complicated because there was a large family, half of whom were estranged and living in far-flung spots all over the world. Knowing I was struggling to make ends meet, working as a waitress in London, Amber's parents offered it to me, for a nominal monthly rent, as long as I'd move out with two months' notice when they asked.

I lived there for two years.

I met Jake in a pub on the corner of Ladbroke Grove and Westbourne Park Road. I was meeting a friend from the restaurant, another waitress. She'd suggested we go watch her friend's band that was playing a gig there. She was late. I was sitting at the bar. He walked in and it was a good thing I was sitting down because my knees went to mush. There was something about him. I felt that familiar electric charge run through me as soon as I saw him. At that time, I still called it "love at first sight". I didn't know it was my Broken Soul Detector going haywire.

He walked up to the bar and leaned on it.

"Wow, what perfume are you wearing?" he asked me.

My radar was oblivious to cheesy lines.

"Paloma Picasso."

'It's very nice." He smiled at me and I was *gone*. "I'm Jake."

"Jessica," I said. This was it… the "J"s finally meet! My heart was pounding. I had this thing, this premonition that my guy, my destiny, would also be a "J". This was absolutely, *definitely* the ONE!

"Are you on your own?" Jake asked me.

"I'm meeting my friend Chloe. We're seeing her friend's band."

"I know Chloe," Jake said, grinning.

"Really?" *Why would she have kept me from my one true love*

175

all this time? "So do you know the band as well?" I asked, innocently.

"Well, I am the band," said Jake.

There you go. That's how you seal the deal. (If you're a guy… and you were wondering how to get the girl… *be the band*.)

Jake was the band for sure. He was the most mesmerising front man I'd ever seen. Sure there were other musicians on that stage but all you could see was Jake (All *I* could see was Jake.)

Years later, when I understood much more about the tortured souls of artists and the allure of drugs to them, and the slow descent into addiction, I understood so much more about what made Jake so charismatic; what makes so many performers so charismatic… basically, *they have so many holes in their bucket you can see right through into their souls and it is electrifying.* But that night, all I was aware of was the way he looked at me through almost every song.

Chloe never actually showed up. And I felt it was something of a blessing. I was star struck. This was absolutely *the one*!

We went to Jake's flat on Lonsdale Road and lay on his bed drinking tea and talking until 5am. He didn't drink alcohol of course (slippery slope to a line and then a pill and then the really dark stuff, he explained). He was about to celebrate being one year clean and sober. *A guy who didn't drink*! I was beside myself. And boy could he *talk*. Well, of course he could talk, he'd just been through six months of intense rehab followed by another six months in a halfway house; all he'd done for a whole year was talk about his feelings.

But I'd never met a boy who could do that. I thought all my Christmases had come at once.

As the sun began to rise, we kissed. It was perfect. And we undressed and we were about to *do it*, and I happened to mention it was my first time, and... *finito*. He pulled away from me. No, no can do, Jake declared. I was too special, he said. He didn't want to be my first, he said. He wasn't worthy of that, he said. If I'd slept with a few men previously, and this was just a one-night-maybe-see-where-it-goes kind of thing, fine, but no... no way, he wasn't prepared to be my first.

My heart was destroyed. I actually begged him, but he was adamant.

I was so embarrassed. I got dressed quickly and walked home.

But, wait, you said he was *your first*, you say. Yes... stay with me here.

I spent the next few weeks in mourning. I pined for Jake. I lost that waitressing job because I didn't show up for two days while I nursed my broken heart. I managed to get a few temping assignments. I was looking for real jobs, but with no real enthusiasm. All I really wanted to do was go to drama school and act for the rest of my life. (But that's another story for another day.)

Then Chloe (who I hadn't seen since before the gig because I hadn't gone back to that restaurant) invited me to a party she was having in the huge house in Camden she shared with seven others.

Surely Jake would be there.

Suddenly I had a plan.

★

He didn't show up until long past midnight. But when he walked in, it was like the Northern Lights had shown up. A colourful, magical, mysterious energy entered the room. I was in a corner talking to someone uninteresting. I saw Jake notice me. I didn't move. I was sipping a diet coke. I hadn't drunk a drop of alcohol. It was part of the plan.

Finally, he came over.

"Hi," he said, gently, touching my arm. "I hoped you'd be here. I didn't know how to get in touch with you." *You could have asked Chloe for my number.* But I didn't say that, that wasn't the plan. I just smiled as he carried on, "I feel like I should say sorry. I shouldn't have let things go as far as they did. You're an amazing girl. You deserve better than me."

"Listen," I purred, with a hint of calculated condescension. (To hell with drama school, I'd do my acting out here in the real world.) *"I'm* the one who should be saying sorry. I sold you a completely fake version of me. I'm not this little Goody Two-Shoes who's never taken drugs. I'm not a virgin. I was just saying all that stuff to impress you. I don't know why. Perhaps because I *want* it to be true? I haven't had the opportunity to go through rehab like you, I had to get off all the drugs and sex on my own, and I did that by kind of making up a new, clean persona. You have every right to hate me. I just needed to come clean. *You* deserve better than *me."* This last sentence delivered with dramatic irony worthy of an Oscar.

Well, it worked. All that chemistry that we'd had lying on Jake's bed talking until the sun came up whooshed back into the space between us. He didn't say anything; he just started kissing me. And we couldn't stop. Our hands were all over each other.

178

"Shall we go upstairs," I said.

He followed me up to Chloe's room. It was in the attic. And we fucked.

I am really sorry to say that it was the most meaningless, cold experience I'd ever had in my life. As soon as we were actually doing the deed, it was nothing. He was a dead weight on top of me, thrusting into me with no rhythm, no panache, no emotion, nothing.

Where were the Northern Lights now?

And for me it was just an act. I just got on with it. I'd tricked him into it. I felt like shit. I thought I couldn't feel worse.

And then Chloe walked in.

The words YOU FUCKING BASTARD! IN MY FUCKING BED… WITH MY FUCKING FRIEND! I AM LITERALLY GOING TO KILL YOU rang in my ears for months.

The reason Chloe hadn't come to the gig that night was because she'd been in a relationship with Jake on and off since they were 16 and he'd just broken up with her. Again. I don't know why she hadn't told me. I guess we weren't as close as I thought… until we were way *too* close for comfort.

"Walk of shame" doesn't even begin to describe what I did when I walked home – all four miles from Camden Town to Notting Hill – that night.

I spent another two days in bed, crying. Then I went to the doctor to ask to be put on the pill. I thought I might as well, seeing as I was now having sex… well… that I might as *well* be having sex, since I'd blown my chance of waiting for my forever guy.

The doctor offered me a prescription of a "completely safe, non-addictive anti-depressant".

In a moment of extreme lucidity, I said, "I'm not depressed, I'm crying for normal reasons, I got my heart broken, I don't need drugs, I'll get over it in a few days, so no thank you very much, just put me on the pill, please."

And I did – sort of – get over it, because someone found my broken soul and tried to love it. It was that first proper boyfriend I had, the one I couldn't fall in love with because he wasn't broken. We stayed together for three years until that miserable moment I broke his heart.

Then there were others, who lasted anywhere from one night to two years… and a pattern definitely emerged. The more broken they were, the more in love I fell. The most recent ex (the one I'd been grieving over for a year, because, after five years together, I genuinely believed I would stay with him forever despite, or maybe *because* he was clinically depressed and unfixable, which meant I could die trying to fix him) had told me the very first night I met him that he'd attempted suicide twice.

But here's the thing… no matter how broken they were, none of them ever complained about my thighs. *None of them*. So why had Rupert's poison stuck for so many years, like a stubborn clot in my self-worth circulation system?

The only other time anyone mentioned the size of my body (and even then only indirectly) was when I lived with a neurotic, passive aggressive actress during my second incarnation in Los Angeles. She was desperate to be a size zero, convinced it would get her more roles (sadly, she was probably right). There was nothing size zero about her but

180

it was what she wanted and she assumed the whole world wanted the same thing.

"Wait," she would say as I was leaving for a meeting. "Let me lend you something. I have a jacket that would look great with that outfit. It hides *everything*."

She tried every diet under the sun and I would frequently be dragged onto them, too. "We *have* to do this juice fast, Debra Messing swears by it."

Once, when she was at her absolute thinnest (she'd managed to drop from a size 6 to a size 2) she went up against Hilary Swank for a role and was told by her manager that the producers said she was 10lb too heavy. She started dieting again. She was going to therapy all this time, had been going for years. Maybe the therapist had skipped the "spotting signs of body dysmorphia" class, or enjoyed the income too much.

As I said before: good therapist... needle in haystack, etc.

There was no getting away from the fact that I had big legs and quite a sizeable bum. But so did Marilyn Monroe, arguably one of the most iconic sex symbols who ever lived. But the girls at school didn't want to be Marilyn; they wanted to be Twiggy. And my roommate wanted to be Keira Knightly (having reasoned that it was the size of Keira's body that got her the roles).

In little acts, later to become known as "fat shaming", they had all pretty much projected their own self-loathing and body dysmorphia onto me.

That first therapist I saw (the pretty good one) told me that when people say or do mean things it has absolutely nothing to do with you. She said the way people treat you is a direct reflection of how they feel inside. If they are mean, they are using you as a punch bag, because they can't get to their own pain. The worse they feel about themselves, the meaner they are.

And there was some hope in that, because one thing I knew for sure was that I'd never been purposely mean to anyone. I was certain I'd been the source of annoyance to many people, and offended people left, right and centre, but never with *intention*, and that was the difference. And on that front, at least, there was a flicker of hope that perhaps, deep down, further down than I could yet see, there was a part of me that had a little bit of love for me. Even if I did have to fight my way through the forest of brambles and thorns that surrounded it like the one around Sleeping Beauty's enchanted castle.

If our choices in life – what we say and do, who we hang out with, where we choose to go – reflect how we feel about ourselves deep down, then I'd made a big bulging bag of bad ones, but I'd also made some good ones. Like taking myself to a healing centre, where something had shifted in me and released a flood of grief.

Yes, I had known for some time that bullies were not to be listened to, but now I had discovered that my legs hadn't got the memo and had been halting the recovery process.

Time I had words with them.

So, as stupid as it sounded, I put the Reiki lady's words into practice. I tried to "make friends" with my thighs.

One Saturday morning, a few weeks after the healing centre episode (after which I'd been feeling surprisingly lighter), I lay in bed waiting until Patrick left for the gym, then I sat up and took my pyjamas off. I looked down at my legs and said,

"I'm sorry for listening to all the horrible things people said about you."

Nothing.

I had a feeling this was going to be a one-sided relationship.

I got out of bed and stood in front of the full-length mirror. I tried to silence the voice in my head that immediately said, "Ugh! You're disgusting!"

I looked at the little scar on my inner thigh that still remained from that sledding accident. Like my chin scar, and neck scar, and all the scars inside my heart, it was a part of my history. I hated those scars.

But our scars make us what we are.

My neck scar reminded me I was lucky to be alive. It reminded me that my mother's quick actions – to fill a bucket with cold water and submerge me in it – had saved me from skin grafts and possibly worse. My inner thigh scar reminded me that my need for attention could result in serious injury. And what was my chin scar a reminder of? I touched it and cast my mind back and suddenly it all came back to me.

How strange.

I gave myself a little wistful smile through the tears that started falling.

My *chin* scar was a reminder of *how much I hated my thighs*.

The morning after that awful night in Portugal, I'd woken up early. I'd put my bikini on and gone out to lie by the pool while it was safe. I was mortified at the idea that the boys had been talking about how awful my body looked (with hindsight, I'm sure they hadn't been, it was probably just Rupert making things up to terrorise me), but I was sure no one would be up for hours; they'd only just got in.

I was terrified of seeing Rupert again. I'd lain in my bed tossing and turning the night before, desperate for the others to get back. But the house had been so quiet. I half wondered whether he'd walked into town and gone to a bar (perhaps to find what he was looking for) or taken a taxi to meet the others. But I couldn't be sure and I certainly wasn't going to leave my room to check.

Dawn had broken that morning on a beautiful day, boasting an azure sky without a cloud in sight. The sun was still low on the eastern horizon so the temperature hadn't reached scorching yet, but it was still warm. It was my last day and I wanted to soak up as many rays as possible.

I must have dozed off because suddenly I heard voices. Male voice. Absolutely paranoid that someone was coming outside and would see my unsightly body I leapt off the sun bed and did a forward dive into the pool.

As my chin clunked hard and loud on the bottom, I cursed myself for not thinking this through. I'd been lying by the shallow end so there wasn't much water for me to dive into. I emerged feeling a little dizzy and nauseous but there was only a dull pain. It wasn't until one of the girls – who had just walked out, still half asleep, onto the terrace – screamed, that I realized something must be very wrong. I looked down at the torrent of blood streaming down my body and floating away in expanding rivulets across the surface of the pool.

I probably could have done with a stitch or two, but I wouldn't let them take me to the hospital. I just lay in my room for the next twenty-four hours, soaking my way through several rolls of toilet paper. I missed the final night's celebrations, which was a huge relief. I never wanted to see Rupert as long as I lived. And because I took a taxi to the airport earlier than the others on the last morning (because I was on a different flight), and because Rupert was killed in a freak skiing accident five years after that (he cracked his head on a tree and, like Natasha Richardson, was initially oblivious of the internal bleeding on his brain, which killed him two days later after he was flown to a hospital in Zurich with a severe headache)… I never did.

Thinking about Rupert, and how devastated his friends and family must have been, put things in perspective for a moment.

At least none of my scars had killed me.

My scars also symbolised survival.

I took a moment to feel grateful for that.

The key, I decided, to a renewed relationship with my body, was to spend more time naked, to have regular "naked time". And I would start immediately.

I walked out into the kitchen… naked. I put the coffee on… naked. I went to take a shower while the coffee was brewing.

I got out of the shower, dried myself and hung my towel on the towel rail. I walked out of the bathroom as I'd walked into it… naked (my bath robe was thus still hanging on the back of my bedroom door), so as I walked out of that bathroom, I *exposed my naked body, fully frontal, to Patrick*.

I have *no* idea why he was suddenly at home, an hour after leaving the house, breaking a schedule that was almost military in precision, and I had no interest in finding out. I just needed to find a new place to live. *Pronto*.

I put word out.

When I emailed Patrick to tell him I had to leave because I had to move back to London suddenly (*just say anything that he can't challenge* I thought), he wrote back with just one word: *okay*.

"The first thing I've got to do," said Alice to herself, as she wandered about in the wood, "is to grow to my right size again; and the second thing is to find my way into that lovely garden. I think that will be the best plan."

Alice's Adventures in Wonderland,
Chapter 4

LEWIS CARROLL

CHAPTER NINE

The Girl Who Took Herself Dancing

Well, that's something you can't do solo. Or can you?

In my desperation to get out of Patrick's apartment as soon as humanly possible, I'd put the word out far and wide, and made it sound way more dramatic than it really was: *need to move out of my place fast, major problem with roommate, can't explain, anything you know of, please forward me. I'll house sit, pet sit, go over my budget or even out of state at this point.* Within twenty-four hours, I was covered for at least the next six months.

I felt a little guilty making people think I was potentially at risk from a murderous roomie, but such was my horror at the thought of ever seeing his face again.

My first stop was a week in Santa Monica. A friend of Greg's lived in an adorable, rustic guesthouse that he rented off an elderly couple who had lived in the area their whole lives. He paid a reduced rent in return for tending the garden and fulfilling other light maintenance duties. When he went on vacation, which was infrequent, he had to get someone to house sit and take over his chores. It was pretty easy stuff, checking the sprinkler system came on, watering the potted plants, bringing in the mail, putting the garbage cans out on the street on the designated day and bringing them back onto the drive again. Stuff I was happy to do.

Then a woman Natalie knew from law school got in touch with me. She was working on a big acquisition, which required her to be based in Sydney for a few months. She wanted to rent out her house (for a very reasonable sum) to someone who would also take care of her cats. I'm not generally a cat person, but a whole house to myself for four or five months? I jumped on it. Even though it was located in yet another place I'd never heard of. She wasn't leaving for a couple of months, but I was welcome to move my stuff in whenever I wanted, and move in whenever it suited me as long as I was in and on cat duty before she left, she said. And between Santa Monica and then, another of Natalie's law school buddies needed a dog sitter for a week *in New York*, my favourite place in the world.

My luck had finally shifted!

As I approached Santa Monica, crawling along the 10 Freeway in slow-moving traffic, approaching the Lincoln off-ramp, I realized I hadn't been down there since that weird meditation session that had kicked off this whole unnerving journey into my unknown. It reminded me that I still had an outstanding duty: to *date myself*. I needed to get back to it, but this time maybe show myself some true love and respect.

If I followed my analogy that dating yourself is like an arranged marriage then I better get on with getting used to it, I thought. Most of my long-term relationships had started with falling in love (or at least lust); this one had started with a questionable idea, that had turned into a drag, that had turned into an obligation. But, as we know, I am not a quitter.

"Right, you," I said, craning my head to look at myself in the rearview mirror, "I don't love you, in fact I don't even like you very much, but I am stuck with you. It's non-negotiable. So I'm going to fake it until I make it."

My face fell for a moment because this reminded me of Natalie's words when she went through the most awful postpartum episode, when she couldn't feel any love for Stella. She wept and wept as she held this little baby that she had no feeling for. She had to force herself to smile at it and cuddle it and nurse it. Luckily, Natalie's sister, her birthing partner, was a trained psychiatric nurse (one who believed in the value of compassion before drugs) and she got Natalie through it. My dear friend had never talked about it since. And once she got over that period, you'd be hard pressed to find a more genuinely loving mother, but I never forgot the look of fear in her eyes, the fear that she might be unable to love her child, and watching her efforts at faking it. I really couldn't imagine what that would feel like. I remember how hard she worked to get through that and it humbled me. And made me more determined to get there myself, with me.

So I decided to make a real vacation out of my week in Santa Monica.

I was taking myself on a vacation.

That was a nice thing to do for me.

The well-worn guesthouse, that had been patched up here and there, was tiny. There was a single bunk bed over a little chair and desk, at which you had to sit to eat your meals. There was a beanbag in the corner, so you could at least relax to watch TV, which I wasn't the least bit interested in. I preferred to read when I took a vacation. And I wanted to read something stimulating, I'd been completely captivated by Jonathan Franzen's novel, the multi-award winning, Pulitzer Prize finalist, *The Corrections*. So when I spotted a copy of his earlier novel, *Strong Motion*, in a bookstore, I snapped it up. It was perfect… totally engrossing. I devoured it in two days, only mildly disconcerted by the topic of earthquakes.

As I pottered around the house and garden, doing my little duties, a sense of calm washed over me. In some ways I felt as though I'd been through a war, or climbed a mountain and had reached a peaceful plateau. Well aware – thanks to Eckhart Tolle – that *this too shall pass*, I treasured these precious days. Who knew, they could be the calm before a storm.

For some strange reason, in all the years I'd resided in L.A., on and off, I'd never actually swum in the ocean. The reason, I had thought, was because I loved rollerblading so much that any time I could get myself down to the beach, I only wanted to rollerblade for as long as I could, along the substantial bike path that runs the length of beach. Only now did I realize that it probably also owed much to the fact that I was horrified by the thought of showing my body in public. Well, that was a challenge if ever I'd thought of one.

It had been so long since I'd been in any water, when I started looking, I couldn't find a single bikini, so I treated myself to a new one from Target. It was red, and a little big for me, which was good for making me feel less fat.

I'd been in Santa Monica two whole days before I was ready to brave the beach.

That was a lie. I wasn't "ready" at all, but I told myself we were going. There was no getting out of it.

I made an occasion out of it and got myself a fancy picnic. Since I was now living a short walk (the property was on 7th Street just north of Ocean Park Blvd) from Whole Foods in Venice – compared to a 15-minute drive to the nearest Trader Joe's – I was quite aware my grocery budget was set to double.

"Fuck it, I'm on vacation," I figured.

I bought a whole selection of delicious snacks and a couple of beers. I'd also picked up a few beachy things in Target when I'd gone to buy my bikini: a cheap cooler bag, a plastic beach mat that rolled into a little bag and a fun beach umbrella in rainbow stripes.

I packed my beach gear and cooler bag into my backpack – the umbrella came in a convenient carry bag that you could sling over one shoulder – remembering to pack my sunscreen and book (Franzen had now given way to Grisham, I'd never read *The Rainmaker*, and according to Natalie, it was the best). I put my bikini on and threw a t-shirt dress over it. I checked once more that I'd done all my chores and, when I could procrastinate no longer, I walked the few blocks down to the beach along Ocean Park Blvd, throwing a quick glance down 4th Street as I went, remembering, with a little stab of emotion, exactly where I'd parked my car the last time I'd come down here.

I started the long walk down to the water's edge, puzzled by how busy it was, until I remembered it was a Sunday. It was a Sunday in the middle of May and it had been particularly hot that week so it was no wonder people had come down to the ocean to cool off.

When I got to the water's edge it was packed. I found a small patch of sand and laid out my things.

I sat on my beach mat and surveyed my surroundings. Within moments, I felt as if I'd landed in a different country. I saw people I'd never seen before.

I saw normal people.

The problem with L.A. is this... it's very hard to find the *real* Los Angeles. It's all too easy to confuse L.A. with Hollywood (the town not the place) and celebrity. If I had a cent for every person I'd heard say, "Ugh, I hate L.A." in my life, I'd have at least a dollar.

When most people come to Los Angeles – from London, New York, Sydney, Paris, wherever – for the first time, it's usually for a week or so, whether they are coming on vacation or for business. They take a cab from LAX to their hotel in Hollywood (the place) or Santa Monica or Beverly Hills. They spend a day or two getting over the jet lag while they get their bearings and regret not renting a car. They walk three blocks to a Denny's because they want "real American pancakes" and they eat a stack of Denny's pancakes and feel like throwing up for the rest of the night. They buy a Starline Tour, and get on and off a bus for two days, making sure they see the Hollywood Walk of Fame, the Chinese Theater, Rodeo Drive, Santa Monica Pier and the houses (or rather the closed, power-operated gates of the houses) of various celebrities, which all entails a *lot* of sitting in traffic. They spend a day at Universal Studios and wonder how they could spend $100 on "snacks" and still feel hungry. If they've come on business – Hollywood business – they get VIP tickets to Universal, but since anyone can now *buy* VIP passes, they still spend 45 minutes waiting for each ride, which is, admittedly, better than the 90 minutes everyone else waited.

And it's not until they're on the plane flying home that they realize what felt so weird. They didn't *see* anyone. They saw other tourists, they saw shop assistants, and waiters, and cab drivers and hotel porters, they saw actors playing Arnie and Tom Cruise at Universal Studios, and they saw a Mexican guy (they assumed… he was actually from Venezuela) with a leaf blower clearing the leaves away from the hotel pool, that no one swam in. They even saw Superman and the Incredible Hulk outside the Chinese Theater. (If they were lucky, they saw Jesus there.) But they didn't see any *real* people, normal people who lived in Los Angeles. They didn't see anyone who actually lived there out and about on the streets, going about their normal business because they didn't go to any of the places where people do that. They can't quite put their finger on it but the whole trip left them feeling empty. So they write L.A. off, calling it a soulless, fake plastic playground, and vow never to go back.

"We did L.A. last summer," my ex's Cornish aunt told me one Christmas dinner. "We didn't like it."

I'd long since given up defending L.A. because you have to go there, with someone who knows their way around, and really *see* the places where people live in order to appreciate it. It's not a city; it is "a conglomeration of suburbs in search of a city" (a description attributed to many writers, from Aldous Huxley to Dorothy Parker). A nicer way to put it is "an eclectic collection of neighbourhoods that create a colourful patchwork quilt unrivalled by any other city in the world" (a description attributed to me). I maintain no other "city" has as many different elements, is as multicultural or cosmopolitan, has such a startlingly broad socio-economic range or skill diversity. But the very best part of L.A. is that it is – when you make an effort to connect – the most accepting, welcoming place on earth. That's why people have always moved there to follow their dreams, and don't leave. You think it's because Hollywood is there? That's a small part of it, yes, perhaps the initial pull, but it's mostly because hope lives there.

"L.A. is where dreams go to die," someone once said to me.

"Maybe," I replied, "but only because better ones can be born."

The people of L.A. are always looking forwards. So it was the first place you found electric cars, and vegan burger joints, and foraging-based restaurants, and gluten-free bread, and zero-waste companies, and biofuel, and eco-businesses: concepts that took another 20 years to hit the rest of the world.

Los Angeles is the City of Angels; its residents are watched over and protected, no matter how bad things get. Even when there is death and destruction, people come together in droves to support each other. L.A. is built on community. Whatever you are for or against, you will find a community that shares your beliefs. So what better place to be in, when you realize you don't really fit in anywhere else in the world, when you're a little bit of a lost soul, when you're just trying to find yourself, and get to know yourself better?

I don't know what I was expecting to see on the beach that day – maybe a scene from *Baywatch*, maybe Nicole Richie and Paris Hilton in their skimpy bikinis – but whatever I'd dreaded, it wasn't there.

There were skinny women, sure, but there were also big, curvy ladies. There were women with big boobs, women with small boobs, tall women, short women, old women, young women, women with three spare tyres of fat hanging over their bikini bottoms. Where had all these women been hiding while I had felt all alone in L.A. with my less-than-perfect figure? I saw women with creamy skin, I saw women with blotchy skin, I saw women with caramel coloured skin and women with skin the colour of dark chocolate. I saw women with pink sunburnt skin. I saw hairy women, I saw women with cellulite and stretch marks. I saw colourful tapestries of varicose veins and spider veins. I saw toenails with fungus and heels with dry, cracked skin. I saw big-bottomed girls and no-bottomed girls.

I felt at home at last.

Of course I saw men and children, too, but mostly I was looking at the women. And I thought of the desperate actresses who would be lining the corridors outside casting offices come Monday morning, girls who hadn't eaten carbs in over five years and had only sipped water for the past two days. And I felt sad that they had forgotten what the real world looked like. I wished I could round them up and bring them all down here.

I took my dress off, stretched my towel over my mat and lay on my front, letting the strong rays of the mid-afternoon sun warm my back. I read for a while and as soon as I felt uncomfortably hot, I got up to go and brave the water. I asked a sweet young couple next to me to watch my stuff.

I was a little apprehensive. The waves looked aggressive, but there were several young children splashing about in them so they couldn't be that scary. As the first one crashed into me I laughed out loud. It was fantastic. I'd forgotten how much fun waves were, how the effort of jumping over them and the thrill of trying to body surf on them was all consuming while you were at it. I'd forgotten how restorative water is, how simply floating in the shallows can make your troubles melt away. I rubbed my skin so that the salt could naturally exfoliate it.

I swam out far, completely out of my depth, and turned to look back at the shore, and the Santa Monica city skyline beyond, slightly to my left. What a place. All the years I'd lived in and around this city and I'd never done this. I shook my head in disbelief. All because what? A boy had teased me? A boy who clearly had a strange obsession with me was determined to traumatise me rather than be rejected by me?

It's wrong to think ill of the dead, I know, but I was mad at Rupert in that moment, for robbing me of so many years of doing *this*.

As I walked out of the water, some droplets of it still clinging to my now glistening body I wished, for one moment, that I wasn't alone. I just wanted someone to share this observation with. Maybe this solo vacation was going to be harder than I thought. The novelty of going to dinner alone, or for a drink solo was one thing; these occasions just entailed spending a few hours in my own company. Now I was asking myself to spend a whole week's vacation alone. This was *hard-core alone time*.

At least in a real arranged marriage there was someone to talk to.

198

I tried not to think about it as I lay on my towel, drying off. I let Grisham distract me. You are never quite alone with a good book.

Overnight, the beach became my new favourite place to hang out in L.A. I couldn't believe what I'd been missing.

There is nothing like the feeling of lying on warm sand, with all your troubles (literally) behind you, staring at nothing but blue sky and blue ocean, listening to waves periodically crashing on the shore against the muted sounds of children playing. It soothed my soul. And with all that sun and salt, my skin began to glow and feel like velvet.

What had stopped me from making the most of this luxurious location in the past? Had it really simply been the fear of exposing my body in public? I remembered how a WASPy girl at the very first company I'd worked at in L.A. had once made some inane comment that "only tourists and Mexicans go to the beach in Los Angeles" when I'd suggested a group trip to the beach, but that couldn't have stuck for all these years. No, it was true, I was simply mortified by the idea of people seeing my thighs. Sure, I'd been on plenty of vacations before, and I guess I always got into a bikini at some point, but these were all in locations where I was pretty sure I couldn't possibly meet someone I knew, and usually with boyfriends who'd already seen me naked. Yes, it was clearly the thought of exposing my legs on a beach in a city filled with size zero actresses that had hampered me.

But it wasn't going to hamper me any longer; I was determined to make up for lost time and spent virtually all day, every day, on the beach.

*

One day I arrived back form the beach and went to check on my car, which was parked on a street a block and a half from the house – I hadn't driven it for a few days and I needed to be sure which side it was on in case I needed to move it for street cleaning.

As I approached, I saw something had been tucked under the windshield wiper. I prayed it wasn't a ticket. It wasn't; it was a leaflet advertising a salsa night at a club above a local restaurant that night.

Salsa dancing. Well, that's something you can't do solo.

Or can you?

The restaurant was a massive Asian fusion place on 3rd Street Promenade. I'd been there once, with Max. He'd taught me – yes, literally taught me – to drink martinis. He ordered me a dirty martini and coached me how to sip it in tiny amounts, with your tongue pressed almost completely against the roof so that it didn't go down too fast and burn your throat. After two he told me the joke that had won me points on dates ever since.

Why are martinis like breasts?

Two are never enough. Three are too many.

I wisely decided against the martinis as I took a stool at the bar in the little club at the back of the restaurant and up a spiral staircase, and ordered a vodka tonic.

The band looked like they were just about to start a set. People were standing around on the dance floor waiting to begin. A stocky man came over and offered me his hand. I raised my palm up to indicate no. He looked puzzled. I didn't know then, but soon saw through observing, that people didn't stick to the same partners, they regularly switched. Men invited women to dance and women accepted. No one refused a dance. You came here to dance. The point was to dance.

But I was on a very special date. We were just patching things up after a bit of a bumpy patch. I wouldn't have felt right dancing with someone else.

I drank the whole of my second vodka tonic before I even considered dancing. (Incidentally, I had experienced another first that evening; I'd come on the Big Blue Bus, along Lincoln and 4th, getting off at Santa Monica, wondering who on earth had started the trend of not using public transport in L.A. Sure, it didn't go everywhere you needed it to, but there was no reason not to use it when you could. But none of us ever did. I vowed to incorporate it into my life more often.)

I turned down six or seven men, all of them looking increasingly confused over what I was doing there if I hadn't come to dance.

Finally, I could not delay my *pas seul* any longer.

I got to my feet after the last number ended and everyone paused for a breath and to applaud the band. I shuffled towards the edge of the dance floor and before I knew it, the band was playing again and I swear it was twice as fast as the last number. People whooped with joy as they took their partners and started twirling around the floor.

Shit!

Well, there was no going back. I'd just have to figure it out.

I actually closed my eyes for a few moments while I tried to let the rhythm get inside me. I shifted my hips from side to side and then, opening my eyes, I started stepping forward and backwards, as I'd seen people do.

It didn't take long before I was really moving. Next I got my arms into the rhythm of it, twisting my wrists around in time to the music. Round and back, back and round, first to the left, then to the right, left, right, left, right. Fantastic! I was ecstatic. I was back in the swing with my body. I felt like I had woken parts of me that had been paralysed for years.

Soon I was weaving in and out of other dancers, in my own little world. At one point I caught sight of the first man who'd approached me. He was taking a break (a well-earned one, he hadn't stopped dancing since I'd turned him down) and was standing by the bar. He watched me, clearly amused. Once more he indicated his hand – was I interested in a partner? Once more I turned him down, but I grinned at him and he gave me a massive smile back.

The song came to an end and I took my seat back at the bar in order to catch my breath and order some water. My jilted partner came over to me.

"Hey miss, I never see a lady dance salsa alone before. You brave lady."

"Yes," I heaved, still desperately trying to catch my breath.

I did suddenly feel brave. I hadn't felt brave in a long time.

When I got home that night, I showered off the sweat I'd worked up in the salsa club; I'd ended up dancing until the very last song.

I dried myself and, before putting my pyjamas on, I sat on the little bunk bed – my head nearly touching the ceiling – and looked down at my naked body. What a privilege, I suddenly thought, to be 100% able-bodied. How many people in the world would love to have all their limbs intact and/or be able to function without impediment? How had I let some random people I'd crossed paths with – not even people who were particularly important to me, in fact quite the opposite – shift my perspective to the point where I had nothing but contempt for my body and felt only disgust when I looked at it.

I brought my thighs up to my chest, wrapped my arms around my shins, and kissed my knees.

How long did it take to fix a leaky bucket?

The next day, still on a high from all that dancing, and feeling like I could take on any challenge, I felt inspired to do something else I'd never done alone. I decided to take a road trip.

I completed my morning chores, put all my beach paraphernalia and a picnic into my trunk and got in my car. I put my "driving compilation" playlist on the car stereo and as I motored up the Pacific Coast Highway towards Malibu, singing U2's 'Where the Streets Have No Name' at the top of my voice, I couldn't have been happier.

The furthest I'd ever been up the PCH before was to Malibu Country Mart, which sits above Malibu Lagoon and in the shadow of Pepperdine University. The ex and I once drove up to Santa Barbara but we'd taken the inland route up the 101.

As I drove on past Malibu Country Mart, towards Paradise Cove and Point Dume, both places I'd heard of but had never visited, I got a little thrill. I was on an adventure. No one knew where I was. It was just me and the road.

Soon, I came to Zuma beach. Now I really felt well and

truly out of L.A., this stunning expanse of sand could have been a stretch of beach anywhere in the world. The sand was golden and softer than the sand in Santa Monica. The dunes made it feel rustic and wild. There were little groups of people dotted around and a lot of surfers in the water. Though the day was exceptionally warm and sunny, the surf was impressive.

I parked up and took my little picnic and my book down to the water's edge. I was on top of the world. I sat there, listening to the waves and watching the surfers, thinking *everyone* should have a go at this. This dating yourself. It's great! You can do whatever you want, stay as long as you want, leave when you want. You're free to soak up your surroundings at leisure… in peace… it's *awesome*.

When I'd had enough food and sun, I got back in the car and carried on driving. What new hideaways would I discover next? I passed more beaches and then got into a stretch of wilderness where there was dry brown brush land on one side and overhead power lines on the other. It felt like the road was kind of hanging over the ocean. Not much to see.

It'll get better soon, I thought.

But it kept on like that for some time.

Just as I was getting a bit irritated that it wasn't getting prettier, the road veered off to the north and… I lost the beach completely! It just disappeared off to the west while the road took me north.

Hey! Beach! Come back!

Now I was driving beside lots of factories and plantations and there were signs for a naval base. No! No, no, no, no, no. This was not what I had ordered. Okay, I hadn't looked at a map, I thought I could wing it, but surely PCH just

204

carried on being beautiful, winding along next to beautiful beaches all the way up to heaven. No?

No.

I turned off PCH to try and find my way back to the beach. But every road I tried was blocked off by the naval base, which separated me from the coast. I was getting really fed up. I got completely lost. (Now, this had been any one of my previous boyfriends getting us completely lost, I would have been losing my shit with him by now, but, damn it, I only had myself to shout at.) At one point I thought I was never going to find my way back to PCH. Finally I got myself back on it and carried on until I found myself on the outskirts of downtown Oxnard. I stopped at a gas station to pee. I'd been in the car for a couple of hours. The sky had turned grey. June gloom was rolling in early this year. Perfect!

Now all I wanted to do was turn around to my other half and say, "I'm beat, honey, will you drive back?" But alas, my honey was me.

I got back in the car sulking, and didn't speak to myself all the way home.

If this was what an arranged marriage was like I wasn't up for it; I wanted a refund.

Damn! This was *hard*.

But as I got into bed I asked myself something: had I ever been in a relationship that had been perfect and smooth sailing in every moment? No. Of course I hadn't.

"Sorry," I muttered to myself.

(Because my first boyfriend's dad had taught us never to go to sleep on an argument.)

She generally gave herself good advice
(though she very seldom followed it).

Alice's Adventures in Wonderland,
Chapter 4

LEWIS CARROLL

CHAPTER TEN

The Girl Who Fell in Love Again

At 9am, I met the new love of my life.

The first time I ever felt love, I mean love for the *person* I was, not dutiful, possessive love because I was someone's child or grandchild or niece or sister, was when I arrived in New York. I was eight years old.

I vividly remember driving across Queensboro Bridge in the cab, my nose pressed to the window, watching the Manhattan skyline getting closer and closer. I painted pictures of that skyline for years afterwards. It spoke to me that skyline, it said, "Welcome home, this is where you belong, everyone here loves you and all your dreams will come true."

At that point in my life, my only true dream was that my parents would stop screaming at each other all day long. That dream could not be accommodated but Manhattan sure showed me a good time and promised I would always be welcome there, and that any *future*, more *realistic* dream would be no problem, no problem at all.

Everyone in New York loved me. The bellboys loved me, the waitresses loved me, the cab drivers loved me, the lady in the Statue of Liberty ticket office loved me. Even the *dogs* seemed to smile at me. For the first time in my little life the bitter squabbling of my parents drifted into the background and I could only hear the sounds of the city (the best New York could do with respect to that immediate dream).

What I was picking up on, at such a tender age, was the New York spirit. In New York everyone is loud. Loud and proud. You don't apologise for who you are or what you want. No one in New York forgets that they are a city, a *country*, mostly made up of people descended from immigrants. Those who arrived into the Upper Bay of the Hudson River, who wanted to remember their origins, remained under the watchful eye of Lady Liberty, who never let them forget their fortune at having been welcomed into this land of opportunity. Those who went south and west most likely forgot.

My clearest memory from that first trip is going to Windows of the World at the top of the North Tower of the World Trade Center. We ate burgers and *fries* as we learnt to say if we wanted to order chips. We got our photo taken and digitally printed onto a tea towel (that I think my mother may still have). We stared out of the observation window and marvelled at the cars below that looked like trails of ants moving around the city grid.

My heart broke on September 11th, 2001, not only in horror and disbelief at the level of violence perpetrated, and the horrific loss of innocent lives, but also because the site of one of my earliest, most precious memories was simultaneously wiped off the map.

By the time I returned to New York, eleven years later, I had become slightly obsessed with the place. My favourite film was *West Side Story*, followed by *Fame*, followed by *Breakfast at Tiffany's* (which I didn't understand properly for another ten years). *Working Girl* and *When Harry Met Sally* also had special places in my heart.

My second trip was an invitation from Courtney Kaplan, the American girl who'd been at our school for a year. I was kind of surprised to get the invite to be honest, especially as it was two years since I'd seen her. She was perfectly pleasant to all of us at school, but she was aloof, she had held us all at arm's length. I wasn't aware that she'd extended an invitation to anyone else from school, so why me? And when I arrived at the awesome Upper West Side apartment she shared with three college friends, she didn't seem too interested in talking about our old school at all. The reason she'd invited me actually came as a bolt out of the blue.

"I think you should apply. For my theater program at NYU," she blurted out half an hour after I arrived, when I hadn't even finished my first New York Cup o' Joe. "You were easily the best actress at school, you should be on it." Adding, before I could process the compliment, "Everyone wants to go to RADA in the UK and here it's Carnegie Mellon or Julliard, but I promise you Tisch is the best," as if I had been weighing up these options and discussing the matter with her for some time.

Several years later, I encountered Courtney's mother – who had morphed into a manager of several big-name movie stars – in L.A. I'd never met the woman before, but I knew who she was. I'd never met anyone more aloof and controlling. It made sense of Courtney's behaviour. I could imagine her as a kid, growing up in this high pressure, Hollywood environment, where everything and everyone is a project not a person.

It seemed Courtney had also been talking me up to the director of the "program". He greeted me as if I was set to enrol that very afternoon. I met everybody. They were all super nice to me (see… this was New York showing me it would make all my dreams come true.) I did an audition; Courtney coached me. They loved me. It was really quite surreal until it started to feel like a real possibility that I would give up my degree in Economics in London and move to New York in "the fall", a real possibility, that is, until it became evident that the fees would be around $30,000 and that I'd need another $30,000 in the bank in order to qualify for the student visa.

By the time I discovered exactly how much it was going to cost, I was back in London. The dream felt so far removed from that distance, I got over it pretty quickly.

As for Courtney, she never became an actress, she moved to Dallas to marry a billionaire and became a Republican.

We lost touch.

There were subsequent visits to New York over the years, to visit various friends who landed jobs there, or to meet the ex for a weekend during the times I was based in L.A. and he was based in London. Every time I was there, every fibre of my being fizzed and sparkled. I was more fun, more attractive, more sassy, more talented, more joyful… more *me*!

It was the perfect place to end my successful year of dating myself (okay seven months, but who was counting), to celebrate the fact that I'd learned to love myself, could survive as a single girl, doing all the things couples do, but on my own. My reward was around the corner. I felt it. I was at the end of my journey and… everyone knows that any decent rom com ends, happily ever after, in New York.

I knew it *in my bones*…
This was where I would meet *the one*!

In true New York style, I wasn't even going to meet Kevin face to face before living in his apartment and taking care of his dog for a week. He'd left on a red eye to Paris the night before. We had emailed to make all the arrangements. I was to pick up the keys from the bar on the corner of Jane and 8th, Kevin's local watering hole. All the instructions were in the apartment. His dog walker had kept the dog for one night and was bringing her to me at 9am the following morning, to introduce us and answer any specific questions I had.

I flew Southwest into La Guardia and treated myself to a cab into the city so that I could approach Manhattan my favourite way, over the Queensboro Bridge. It was 11pm by the time we were approaching so the skyline was lit up. There is nothing, *nothing* in the world so exciting as watching that skyline growing bigger and bigger as you get closer and closer, especially if it's been a while since you've seen it.

The top of my head went all tingly.

When I arrived at the little West Village bar, the bar manager gave me the keys, and a beer on the house, and then I walked down Jane Street to the brownstone building that housed Kevin's apartment. It was all magical. I was in a movie, I was sure of it. The script had been written and everything was going to plan. All I had to do was play my part.

Kevin's studio apartment was insanely tiny but immaculately tidy. In one look I knew Kevin wasn't into women.

So we weren't destined for each other. That was okay. He wasn't the one. I was cool with that. I scratched that idea from my head.

I slept like a baby and was wide awake, despite the three-hour time difference, at 8am. I showered and popped out quickly to get coffee. I was always fascinated by how no one I ever stayed with in New York had coffee making equipment in their apartments, unlike L.A. where most people had three different contraptions (a filter machine, espresso maker and French press) along with 8lb of fresh ground coffee in the freezer. This, I deduced, was because you could get a great cup of coffee at any time of day or night in New York, within a 30-second walk from any residence in the city. With that plus the fact that kitchen counter tops averaged about 12 inches square of surface space, who had the space for a coffee maker?

I loved going out for coffee *all* the time. It felt ridiculously indulgent and yet highly efficient at the same time. With every cup of coffee bought, you felt like you were keeping the economy alive.

At 9am, I met new the love of my life; the new *canine* love of my life at least. Maggie was a perfectly scaled down German Shepherd mixed with whatever breed had shrunk her. She arrived attached to the dog walker, and if Kevin wasn't sleeping with him, he should have been… the guy looked like he'd stepped off a magazine cover.

"How's the modelling career going?" I quipped

"Slowly catching up to the dog walking career," he quipped back, deftly.

He reiterated what Kevin had written on the instructions, that you really couldn't over walk this dog. She loved being out – on the streets, in the park, by the river, it didn't matter, she just loved being out. But she wasn't a pushy pet, she had impeccable manners, she would always wait until she was invited. She was generally very well trained and highly obedient. She only got feisty if she sensed her owner (or *in loco* owner) was fearful.

Within ten minutes of the dog walker leaving, Maggie was curled up at my feet as I sat on the couch/bed reading a magazine. I read, distracted, for about five minutes before I put my hand under her chin and said, "Well I'm not going to meet him sitting in here, am I? Let's go."

Thus began a magical week of mooching around Manhattan with Maggie. We walked the length and breadth of the city. We people watched; we dog watched. We picnicked in Central Park; we walked by the river. We only went home to eat and sleep. I would wear her out in the mornings and then spend my afternoons grocery shopping, visiting museums or browsing bookstores while she napped in the apartment. I'd take her out again for a long walk before dinner. We would generally sit outside at one of the myriad little restaurants along Bleecker.

At the end of May, the weather in New York can be spring or summer. We got lucky; we got spring. It was warm and fresh, never too hot and no humidity to speak of. I couldn't have wished for a better setting to conclude my story. My happy ending was just around the corner. *I could feel it coming.*

I had never felt so at peace. I knew in my heart that the moment was approaching, the moment when I would meet *the one*. The one I had been waiting my whole life for; the one true love of my life. They would know it when they saw me, too, because they had been waiting all this time to meet *me*. They would be by my side forever, loving me and taking care of me. I just knew what it would feel like… it would feel like "coming home" (because that's what everyone said it would feel like.)

My life was about to change forever.

I kept my antennae on high alert.

I didn't want to miss him.

But he proved quite elusive.

I scanned the faces in the crowds wherever we went. I willed Maggie to sniff him out. (*She* will sense him and *that* will be my sign.)

However, he wasn't in Central Park. And he wasn't at MOMA. And he wasn't walking towards us one evening on Bleecker, or listening to the saxophonist in Washington Square. He wasn't in the pasta aisle of the 6th Avenue Trader Joe's and he wasn't at the Strand Bookstore, on any level. He wasn't at the sushi bar in the East Village. I was running out of places.

If *only* I'd known his name, I could have called it out.

I went out one night for a couple of beers at the corner bar on Jane and 8th where I'd picked up Kevin's keys. I met a guy who looked like Al Pacino (if Al Pacino's face had melted slightly after a botched bout of plastic surgery). I really hoped it wasn't him. No, he was married. Didn't stop him hitting on me after a few drinks. The bar manager joined (and kind of took over) our conversation, allowing me a lucky escape.

I felt like Charlotte in *Sex and the City* when she wails, "I've been dating since I was 15, I'm exhausted. Where *is* he?"

I'd been in New York almost a week. Seriously, *where was he*?

216

★

On my final morning in the city I was trying not to panic. I worked hard to convince myself that (obviously) the moment we were destined to meet was coming right at the *end* of my trip, in order to build the suspense and make it all super dramatic in the big climax of my story.

Maggie and I had a little stroll around Central Park after our final picnic there. It was Memorial Day. The park was busy, but there's always room for everyone. Families chilled out with their picnics; the drives were thick with runners, skaters and cyclists. We were making our way out of the park, heading towards Columbus Circle, when Maggie pulled on her lead and veered away from me. This was unusual. She stuck by my side religiously unless we were in a designated dog park and she was off the lead when I would chuck balls – not very far, I throw worse than a girl – for her to fetch. But it seemed she had seen something lying on the path and had felt compelled to investigate. Soon I saw it, too. Something white and red was lying on the path. A piece of paper? A photo? As we approached, I saw it was a playing card, lying face up.

The seven of hearts.

Maggie sniffed it. I picked it up.

The seven of hearts. The *seven*. My lucky number.

I crouched down and pulled Maggie into a hug. She pawed my knee. I kissed the top of her head.

"Yes, girl, this means something. Good girl. Thank you."

And suddenly I knew where to go. *Of course* he'd be there. How could I have been so stupid? How did I forget?

I couldn't get Maggie home fast enough.

★

There was one thing that I had always loved to do in New York that I hadn't yet done on this trip. I discovered it the first weekend the ex and I ever spent in the city. We wanted to do the Statue of Liberty tour but the wait was going to be too long. We got chatting to a woman who said she and her husband were going to ride the Staten Island Ferry across the bay and back instead. Their friends had told them it was infinitely cheaper than paying for the tour and you got a great view.

She was right, it was a great vantage point from which to marvel at the iconic statue. I couldn't even imagine the point of getting much closer. And on the return trip (we literally got off the ferry on Staten Island and lined up to go back on the next) we stood out at the very front. From that position, watching the skyline grow bigger and bigger as we moved in across the water, it felt like we were stationary and the whole of Lower Manhattan was moving towards us.

I loved it so much, and on our next trip I wanted to do it again. The ex said it was boring to do it again. So I left him in a bar watching basketball and went alone. Thus it had become "my thing" and I did it again on my own on our third weekend there (which turned out to be our last, so perhaps there was something prophetic in that.)

I didn't know for sure if dogs were allowed on board, but I decided it best not to take Maggie even if they were.

"Sorry, girl," I said to her as I changed from my jeans and t-shirt into my bright pink dress and put some lipstick on. "This is something I have to do alone. But I'll tell you all about it later."

★

I walked – nay, skipped – all the way over to 7th Avenue and jumped on the 1 train to South Ferry Station. Even on the subway I was checking out every guy in approximately the right age range (which I kept pretty wide to be honest, I didn't want to rule anyone out), but in my heart I knew he wasn't there. I knew where he would be.

He would be on the Staten Island Ferry. I knew it; I just *knew it*. Now everything started to make so much sense. This was the reason the ex hadn't wanted to join me on subsequent trips, he *wasn't meant to be the one with me on the Staten Island Ferry*, even though I had been so sure he was "the one" at the time. No, there was someone in my future I was meant to be with, but I just needed to do some necessary work on myself before I was ready.

Now I was ready!

When I arrived at the terminal, a ferry had just departed so I found myself at the front of the crowd waiting for the next one. As people gathered around, I looked straight ahead at the reflection of the assembling crowd in the huge glass doors that would soon open to let us board the boat. I caught sight of a pretty girl in a pink sundress – with short sleeves, a square neckline and empire waistline – and for a split second I thought to myself, wow, she looks so beautiful.

And then I realized it was *me*!

I know that sounds weird but honestly, just for that first split second that I caught sight of my own reflection, I didn't realize I was looking at myself and I genuinely thought the person I was looking at looked beautiful. And so I knew, right then, for sure, that I had completed my journey, that I genuinely loved myself and had set myself free. I stared at myself, remembering with such sadness how much I used to hate looking at myself in a full-length mirror. Why had I thought I was *so* fat? I was shapely, that was for sure, but I wasn't obese. And even if I was, it wouldn't have been something to be *ashamed* about. Worried, perhaps, for my health, but not *ashamed*. I'd broken those toxic chains that that had held me and tormented me for years. I smiled at myself and then something made me turn around and…

There he was!

Of *course*.

He was… everything. His eyes, that were looking directly at me, were sparkling. He was very tall. Protectively tall. I'd fit my head under that chin perfectly. He had short soft brown hair that was just a little bit wavy. He kept smiling at me. I wasn't scared; it didn't feel weird. In fact, the greatest sense of ease and calm descended on me and I felt enveloped in warmth.

Was he coming over? No. Should I walk over? How were we going to meet? I started to giggle, nervously.

Someone brushed up against me and I stepped aside and looked around at a woman with a baby strapped to her body in a sling. She was making her way along the front row of people, holding her hands out to protect the baby's face as it was facing forward. The baby was cute; it looked around six months old.

"Sorry," she whispered as she passed me, having realized she'd brushed against me.

"That's okay," I said and looked up to see…

She was walking up to *my man*! What?! Nooooo!

The beautiful smile on that man's face was not for me.

Of course it wasn't for me.

It was for his beloved family.

★

My eyes turned hot and heavy as the doors opened and we filed onto the ferry. I walked onto it like a zombie. I cried all the way to Staten Island and back. I had no more faith left in me to believe that I was going to meet "the one" actually on board the ferry. I knew, then, how hard I'd duped myself.

I wasn't sad because a handsome stranger had turned out to belong to somebody else. I was devastated because I wasn't fixed. The bubble burst and I saw what an idiot I'd been; what a *complete* idiot. I'd fallen straight back into my old pattern, assuming that I'd know my true love at first sight.

I still naïvely believed that I could fix my leaky bucket with someone else's love. I had no idea how much patching up I still had to do on my own.

Right then and there, I wanted to give up and abandon that bucket.

But Maggie needed her dinner.

Having managed to hold the tears back on the subway ride home, I cried again immediately as soon as I walked through the apartment door and saw Maggie. I cried over dinner, which was picnic leftovers that I ate sitting on the fire escape. I cried myself to sleep, and I cried like a *baby* when I had to say goodbye to Maggie at 4am as I left to get a cab to the airport to catch my flight.

Dawn was breaking over Manhattan as the Boeing 737 lifted itself off the runway. We took off to the east and the enormous effort the plane put into lifting itself higher and higher represented the enormous effort I knew it would take to lift myself out of this sad hole I'd fallen into.

221

Finally, we banked to the right, the side of the aircraft on which I was sitting. I pressed my face to the window and looked down at the city getting smaller and smaller, my heart breaking as I said goodbye to it.

I lifted my eyes to look out at the western horizon, where we would soon be headed. It was still dark out there. I was going back into darkness. But then a strange thing happened. My eyes suddenly refocused and I was looking at someone.

Of course.

There.

I was looking at *the one*. The one who truly loved me for who I was, the one who had my back, the one who'd take care of me for the rest of my life, the one who'd make mistakes with me, the one I'd forgive and the one who'd forgive me, the one who I now realized I'd known *was* the one the second I set eyes on her.

You see... the seven of hearts hadn't lied to me.

I *had* met the love of my life on the Staten Island Ferry. She was the girl whose reflection I saw in the glass doors. She was *the girl in the pink dress who had smiled at me*!

It was so long since she had been anything near the right size, that it felt quite
strange at first.

Alice's Adventures in Wonderland,
Chapter 5

LEWIS CARROLL

CHAPTER ELEVEN

The Girl Who Found True Love

"It's not you, it's me!"

"When you realize you want to spend the rest of your life with somebody, you want the rest of your life to start as soon as possible," Harry tells Sally. This was just one of several movie quotes about love that I now realized was a complete pile of poop.

I arrived back in L.A. under a darker cloud than I'd ever known. And it wasn't just my mood; June gloom had descended upon us and it wasn't shifting.

For southern California residents, June gloom – a time when thick, grey clouds roll in and the cool air feels heavy and clammy – is a welcome break from the intense heat, scorching sun and unbroken blue skies that prevail for most of spring, summer and fall. But for those of us who hail from British shores, it is a reminder of everything we ran away from.

The realization that dating wasn't just for Christmas, it was for life, knocked the stuffing out of me. I was horrified to discover that I wasn't simply revamping myself ready for the next relationship, babysitting myself until a real grown up took over, dusting out the emotional closets and tossing the skeletons away in order to be worthy of a better lover…

that the point of repairing the bucket wasn't so that it could be filled with someone else's love. No… *I had to fill it myself!*

I was stuck. Stuck with me. *Forever.*

I was *the one*.

FUCK!

I guess I fell into a period of mourning.

On balance, though, I was still treating myself marginally better than I once had. I could easily have taken up smoking again, faced with such a depressing future. But I didn't. And I gave up pasta. No matter how down I felt, I kept up my morning walk every day and even went to yoga occasionally. And my new abode was also a reflection of the higher standards I'd adopted; it was a far cry from the dump beside the 5 Freeway I'd subjected myself to for those few months.

But the honeymoon period was *definitely* over.

Before I went to live in Cypress Park, I had never known (or cared, to be honest) where Riverside Drive went once it crossed the Los Angeles River and headed east. I had only ever used it, where it meets the intersection of the 5 and the 101, to get on or off those freeways. The first time I ventured past the point where it becomes Figueroa was in early May that year, when I'd dropped my things off at my new place, before my couple of house/pet sitting stints in Santa Monica and New York.

Shortly after passing under the freeway tangle and over the deep concrete channel of the so-called Los Angeles "River" (that sports barely a trickle of water at the bottom of it for most of the year, a trickle that turns into a veritable torrent for a few days in the short but intense rainy seasons that infrequently batter the city, when it has unfortunately been known to claim the odd victim in drowning incidents) I was stunned to find the area I was driving through unrecognizable as "L.A." as I knew it.

You would be forgiven for thinking you had crossed the border into Mexico.

I stared out of the car windows at the big grocery stores that lined the street. In place of signs for "Ralphs", "Vons" and "Pavilions" were names I'd never seen before, such as "Super King Market", "Superior Grocers" and "Big Saver Foods". There were billboards and signposts written solely in Spanish. There was an unfamiliar buzz on the streets. I was hearing a different language… a different culture. Families and neighbours crowded around taco trucks, kids weaving in and out of them. Cars stood parked in "no parking" spots that blocked in other drivers who were just waiting around patiently until the owner returned from their errand. No one seemed in any hurry to get anywhere or do anything. Yes, there were sinister looking groups of guys dotted around… all of them dressed in hooded jackets despite the heatwave we were being blasted with that week… all of them in sunglasses, some with bandanas hiding their faces and… is that a gun in your pocket or are you pleased to see me? But I didn't feel uneasy for a second; the vibe on the street was a good one.

The first question I asked the Mad Cat Lady (as she quite happily called herself on account of the fact that for a period of time in her 20s she'd had *four* feline companions) when I arrived was whether this area was home to the Avenues gang that I'd heard about when I'd viewed the room to rent in Glassell Park a few months previously.

"Absolutely," she informed me, with more than a hint of pride. Off my startled look, she explained that, far from this fact making it a dangerous place to live, you'd be hard pressed to find a *safer* neighbourhood in Los Angeles.

"The gangs have turfs," she explained. "They go to neutral territory to settle their disputes. If you live around here, as long as you're not from a rival gang, it's like you're on protected land. I haven't locked my car in the three years I've lived here. I sit on my porch until midnight, chatting to the neighbours' children." To my renewed puzzled expression, she explained, "Oh, the children around here sleep the same schedule as their parents. It's like two shifts: 1am until 7am, after which they have school and work, and then a long siesta from 5pm until around 7pm, when they get up and prepare dinner and enjoy their family time." Lucky kids! Sounded pretty fun to me. "Trust me, you'll love it. It's a whole new world," she promised me.

Thus began my immersion into Mexican culture.

The sweet Mad Cat Lady spent a whole day showing me that whole new world. She took me to South Pasadena… *on the metro*. I'm ashamed to admit I hadn't even been consciously aware of there *being* a metro in L.A. I guess I knew there was one, somewhere in the back of my mind, but I'd never heard of anyone using it so it kind of faded into the back of my mind.

"South Pas" (as she called it) was another revelation in itself; a delightful neighbourhood that welcomes you the second you step off the Gold Line. She showed me her favourite deli and bread shop, and where the yoga studio was, above the organic café. We browsed the arts and crafts materials in the little craft shop, and visited an old-fashioned ice-cream parlor across the street from the public library, which she said she could lend me her account card for.

On the way home from the metro station, she walked me through the neighbourhood a little, pointing out some of the architectural details that hailed from Mexican times.

By the time we got back to the house, I was buzzing with excitement. Just one thing worried me, but it was a little awkward to bring up.

"Look," I said, tentatively to Mad Cat Lady, "This is a difficult question but… will my" – I hated this word – "*colour* be an issue? I feel a little fish out of water."

She laughed.

"You assume I'm Mexican, right?" I nodded. She shook her head, grinning. "I'm Puerto Rican. I'm probably the only legal Latina in the neighbourhood, but because of the colour of my skin, and the way I speak the local Spanish people have assumed I'm Mexican my whole life." I listened to her in awe. "You'll be fine," she reassured me. "Especially with the British accent. Just talk about David Beckham a lot. Wear a Manchester football shirt. They'll love you."

I recoiled. Much as I'd firmly broken with my family's tradition and turned my back on Manchester *City*, in favour of a better team, wearing a Manchester *United* shirt would be a bridge too far. There are some things a girl should not be expected to do, even if she fears for her life. But I didn't explain any of this to her; this is something only British football fans will truly understand.

For the six weeks after I returned from New York, and before she left for Australia, the Mad Cat Lady and I shuffled around each other as respectful housemates. I had never lived with someone in a house they actually owned (as opposed to rented and sub-let to me) and, while she was perfectly charming and hospitable, I found it stressful. Even though I was paying good rent, I couldn't shake the feeling that I was a *guest* rather than a tenant with a right to be comfortable in my own home, so I did lots of apologising when I found her waiting for me to finish in the kitchen and bathroom, and I would disappear for long stretches to the library, for fear of getting in her way.

The rent was reasonable. I mean it was a little more than I'd paid in the past but once Mad Cat Lady left, it was for a whole house. Yes, with cats to take care of, but a *whole house*, with a beautiful garden, with an *avocado* tree in it.

The cats – one black, the other a ginger tabby – were called Fred and Ginger. Unfortunately, it was the black one who was the girl, and because Ginger obviously had to be called Ginger, she had to be called Fred. But I thought "Fred" was a pretty cool name for a girl. And the smartest boy I'd ever met was a red head, so it worked for me.

As I mentioned before, I've never been into cats but these two were so affectionate, so much more like dogs than cats, I started to warm to them. They certainly seemed to like me, even more so after Mad Cat Lady left the building. We all missed her cheerful presence. They became as attached to me as Maggie had been in New York.

Why did animals like me more than I liked me? What did they see that I couldn't or *wouldn't* see?

As the heat that had blasted us through July and August finally gave way to some cooler temperatures in September, I felt my brain begin to take shape again. While the whole industry had been in the South of France, or the Hamptons, or wherever else they go for the summer, I'd been waiting for feedback on the latest draft of the TV pilot that I'd submitted back in late April.

I'd been whiling my days away in the air-conditioned library, fleshing out my idea for the feature film, for which I'd done a little on-the-ground research while I'd been in New York. The topic was dark and thus did nothing to lift my mood, which wasn't so much *low* as it was numb.

What did help my mood a little was discovering the Rose Bowl Aquatics Center, which boasted Olympic swimming and diving training facilities. It had provided much welcome relief from the heat in those summer months. One pool was reserved for length-wise lane swimming, but the other pool, which served the diving boards at the deep end, had horizontal lanes for slower, less ambitious swimmers. It was quite a treat to paddle back and forth whilst watching the dive team practice. The pint-sized pre-pubescent girls, flinging themselves off the highest platform before twisting and turning in the air, and bending in and out of the pike position, reminded me of my gymnast days.

And then that made me feel even more depressed about my body.

I was over it. I was over the effort it took to fake it. I didn't want to date me. I didn't want to date anyone. I just wanted to go back to... what? That was the problem... I'd come too far, I'd lost my innocence, there was no "going back" to a time when I hadn't even *tried* to love myself. I envied anyone who wasn't me, simply because they hadn't pursued this inane quest to "date themselves" as a kind of deluded way to deal with the fact that they knew they were going to end up alone.

All alone.

That was it. That was the pain. I was going to be alone. For the rest of my life. I would never, ever, trust myself to get involved with a man again. If I couldn't make it work with me, what hope had I of making it work with anyone else? And when I looked back over my past relationships, the rose-coloured glasses finally came off. Every so-called "relationship" I'd ever been in was a complete farce. Every one of them was simply a way to avoid being alone... with myself. Actually, I'd date anyone, *anyone* as long as I didn't have to date me. I didn't want to date me if I was the last person on earth.

Why?

Because I was awful; truly awful.

And now here I was... by myself, just as I'd feared.

This weighed on me and needled me until one morning I woke up, about a week before my birthday and it was as if someone had planted the seed of a little thought in my brain, that had grown overnight and was now as clear as day.

Finally, *I got it*!

It all made sense.

I had let my shame win.

All the things about me that I didn't like, all the stupid things I'd ever done, all the aspects of my personality that I didn't like... I was *ashamed* of. And I was letting that define me.

When someone says, "I thought I would die of shame," it's not an exaggerated or inaccurate idiom. Sadly, people do, quite literally, die of shame. They experience some trauma, at some point in their lives – sexual abuse, bullying, financial ruin, loss of social status, divorce, etc. – and they believe that everyone is disgusted with them, ridiculing them, judging them, hating them… literally, everyone: their family, their friends, their colleagues, their *god*, even strangers on the street.

But by "everyone" they really mean themselves, and deep down, they do *know* that, which is why they end up unable to "live with themselves" and either constantly sabotage their wellbeing by indulging in damaging behaviour and substances, or, in the worst cases… by ending their own lives. Or trying to. And they will keep trying to unless they figure out how to *win against those voices of shame*.

She had spoken such truth, that Mexican (although now, who knew, perhaps Puerto Rican) lady in the white Subaru Outback. But I'd only half understood her at the time. Yes, you have to fix your head first of all. You have to figure things out, dredge through the past to get to the source of the shame, understand why you veered off course in the first place. But I assumed, when she had then indicated her heart, that this was all in order to lead you to a much greater love *with another*. But no, see… you fix your head in order to mend your *own* heart.

Because *you're* the one who actually broke your heart, no one else. *You* made the choices, *you* let someone punch those holes in the bucket, *you* failed to fix them before they caused a full-scale water-logging of the foundations leading to major subsidence and the need for an entire remodel.

I'd been doing it all wrong. Loving yourself wasn't just saying, "I love you," or hugging your naked body, or taking yourself on dates, or on a round trip on the Staten Island Ferry because you love it so much.

Loving yourself, for real, is *forgiving yourself*.

Could I forgive myself the years and years I'd felt such intense disgust for myself, the myriad ways in which I'd ridiculed myself, the harsh judgment I'd delivered upon my every action, the hidden hatred I'd harboured for myself?

At this point, the best I could do was try.

And so I stopped saying *"sorry"* and tried *"I forgive you."*

That morning my life changed forever. Not because it became easy, or pain free, or I morphed into a different person and never suffered again, but because I learnt to live with myself... by forgiving myself.

I also promised myself that I would never, ever get into another relationship with someone else until I was in a really good one with myself. I felt like, if all I ever achieved, in my lifetime, was building a good, healthy relationship with myself, even if I never graduated onto building a relationship with someone else, I'd consider that a true success.

So, as my "year of dating myself" drew to a conclusion with my upcoming birthday, I followed the natural course that anyone who'd been dating someone for a year would take. I moved forward.

I moved from *dating* into a *relationship*.

I took the rest of the week off and started making plans. I told my friends I would be out of town for my birthday and we'd have a party when I got back. Technically I wasn't lying. I was physically "out of town" in terms of what anyone considered "town", which didn't generally include gangland.

I started to think of what one does for the person one has agreed to "go steady" with after a fairly shaky year of dating.

A couple of days before my birthday I went shopping. I just wanted one simple (but kind of expensive) gift.

In the five years I'd dated the ex, he'd never bought me a single piece of jewellery. Okay, I had been pretty specific, explaining that I would never wear diamonds, due to the likely human cost of mining them, that I didn't like to wear gold, and that there was really only one place I yearned to own jewellery from…

Tiffany's, of course.

His excuse, year in, year out (not that I pushed the issue much) was that I was too hard to please. But I'd been *very specific*. Silver… simple… no diamonds… Tiffany's. What's so hard about that?

There were plenty of locations to choose from, but I felt the one that would give me the closest experience to being at the iconic New York location would be Rodeo Drive.

Being newly *au fait* with the L.A. public transport system, I decided to park several blocks away and take a bus down Wilshire Boulevard. But I had no luck in the southeast quadrant of Doheny and Wilshire, so I tried going further south but back west a little, and finally ended up finding a spot on Rexford, just north of Pico. I could get the bus up Beverly Drive.

It wasn't until I was out of the car and on Beverly Drive, heading back up to the Pico bus stop that I realized how close I was to Zach's place. I wondered what had become of him in the year since he had ceremoniously dumped me twice. What a sucker I'd been. *Wait*. That was not very kind; I stopped myself short from going down that line of thought.

"I forgive you," I said, so loud and so proud that a woman passing me on the street whipped around in surprise, wondering what she'd done wrong. "No, not you," I reassured her. "Me. I forgive *me*." She gave me an even more perplexed look and went on her way. I smiled to myself.

In Tiffany's I narrowed down my choices. There were not that many, given my self-imposed restrictions and my mini budget, but I had a few good ones. In the end I went for a charming bracelet of tiny silver beads, with the classic heart pendant attached it and engraved with *Please return to Tiffany & Co.* NEW YORK 925. I asked the beautiful sales assistant who'd helped me choose it to gift wrap it.

"Oh, sorry, sweetie," he said emphatically, stroking my arm (again). "I thought it was for you."

"It is," I said, confidently, with a smile. "But it's a gift so I'd like it gift wrapped."

"Oh I *love* your style," he flitted at me as he set about doing the best gift-wrapping job (I am sure) of his life.

I had bought a ticket, for my birthday eve, to a classical concert in Pasadena. A visiting chamber orchestra was performing a program of two Beethoven symphonies: my favourite (the 7th) followed by my second favourite (the 3rd, the "Eroica" – not the "Erotica" as the ex had called it when I took him to hear it once).

I went shopping that morning and purchased a new dress

in Banana Republic (a flattering black and white panelled tunic dress) and a cupcake for later.

We were going through a cold snap (the weather in L.A. can be all over the place in October) so it was cold enough to wear long boots with the little black dress, which was particularly useful since I had decided not to drive, so that I could have a few drinks if I wanted, and the boots were comfortable enough to walk in. I would get the Gold Line to the Del Mar station in Pasadena, from where it was a short-ish walk to the auditorium.

I did my make-up and hair, got dressed, and checked myself out in the mirror. I looked like a woman going out on a birthday date with someone special. I even felt a flutter of excitement. But I was scared. Sitting in a bar or restaurant alone, I could easily pass myself off as someone waiting for a friend, who'd suddenly had to cancel, perhaps. Dancing in a salsa club that I'd probably never visit again was a lark, a gimmick. But going out on a proper, expensive, grown-up date, looking like a proper grown up dressed up for said date… but *with no visible date*? Could I? Really?

I thought back to the salsa club, and then about making a fool of myself in front of ice girl and her friend at barbrix. The voice of shame bubbled up with jeers about how pathetic I was. With considerable effort I stopped it and changed the rhetoric.

"I forgive you for everything," I told the girl in the mirror.

It wasn't easy; I'm not going to lie. The concert hall was filled with couples and small groups, and as I purchased my glass of champagne and moved to the side of the ante-chamber that was being used for the pre-concert reception,

I felt self-conscious. But once the concert started and Beethoven's exquisite music flooded through me, I also thought of all the single people in the world, who didn't have a date, or any friends with a mutual interest in classical music, to go with, who would just *love* to be in my shoes but were too scared to do *this*, to buy a ticket and simply go alone. I was doing this for them, too.

"Thank you," I whispered to myself in the dark, holding my own hand tightly and breathing back the tears of emotion that tried to squeeze themselves out of my eyes.

When the concert was over, I floated back to Del Mar Boulevard on quite a high, not only filled with the joys of being immersed in such beautiful sounds, but also proud of myself for going, and grateful I'd had the courage to take myself.

It was still early, around 10pm (okay, late for L.A. but early for a birthday night out), so I invited myself for a little birthday cocktail at the bistro that was housed in the same building as the metro station.

I told the bartender it was my birthday. He suggested we make up a signature cocktail for me. I told him I liked gin, *good* melon liqueur (not Midori), grapefruit and lime. He made me the best cocktail I'd ever tasted.

He went off to serve other customers and I luxuriated in my personal beverage. It was a short drink and I got through it pretty quickly. I was almost done with it when the bartender appeared at my end of the bar again.

"Of course I was going to buy you your birthday drink," he said. "But the guy at the end of the bar beat me to it. So I'll have to buy you a second one." He looked at my almost empty glass. "I'd say you're ready for it."

It would have been rude to say no... and it *was* my birthday.

I looked over to where the bartender had pointed down the bar and Tim Robbins smiled and waved at me. I nearly fell of my bar stool.

(No, don't kill my fantasy. I *truly* believed, for about ten seconds, that the universe had sent me Tim Robbins for my birthday.)

Tim made his way over, as he got closer looking a little less like the star of my all-time favourite film (*The Shawshank Redemption*) and my teenage crush, but still *very* sexy.

"Thank you for the drink," I said as he approached.

"May I?" He indicated the seat next to me.

"Sure," I said, though not quite sure if this was allowed. Was this cheating? Or bending the rules? Well, I certainly wasn't contemplating getting into a relationship with him. I recalled a married male friend defending his flirtatious ways with that "it doesn't matter where you get your appetite from as long as you eat at home" line. I wasn't sure. Nor was his wife.

"So what's a beautiful girl like you doing on her own on her birthday?" Tim asked.

"Enjoying my own company," I replied breezily.

"Husband out of town?" he asked, and I caught him trying to check out my left hand. I held it out to show there was no ring on it.

"No," I said plainly. "No husband. Or boyfriend. Or girl-friend," I tossed at him, in anticipation of all the usual questions. "Not looking to be in a relationship right now. Just enjoying a little time with myself." I immediately noticed that I'd said *with* myself and not *by* myself.

Tim took all this as an invitation to make a move, which I felt was harmless enough.

So we flirted. It felt nice. It felt *really* nice. I realized how different it felt, flirting with no intention of letting it go any further. Since I had no *need* of him, I felt powerful... more in control. I'd flirted a little with other guys when I'd been in long-term relationships, but I'd always made my off-the-market status very clear. It was interesting to observe the effort Tim made once he knew that I was technically available even if I was saying I was *not* available. He clearly didn't understand what I was doing so he saw me as fair game. But he was cute, and interesting, and funny, and actually began to look more like Tim Robbins the more I drank, so...

I tried to drink my second cocktail slowly (the first had gone to my head a little), letting Tim touch me at his leisure, resting his hand on my leg for a second as he leaned in to say something quietly, tapping me lightly on the arm to emphasise a point. I got a real buzz from it, which mingled with the cocktail. It was kind of disappointing when I had to say, "I'm so sorry, I have to go, I have a date to keep."

"I thought you weren't dating anyone," Tim responded, sharply, looking a little worried. I took a deep breath.

"I... have a date with myself. It's my *actual* birthday tomorrow, so I want to be home by midnight to do something." It was nearly 11.30pm. "There's a train in about five minutes."

"You want to take the metro? On your own? At this time of night?!"

"It's perfectly safe," I assured him, and then laughed, thinking of how I would have reacted a year ago if someone had suggested I do the very thing I was about to do.

"Okay," he announced, getting off his bar stool and standing very close, offering me his hand. He was almost as tall as real Tim. My stomach did a little flip. "I'm walking you to the station."

"It's right there, out the back door," I laughed.

"Then we'll go out the front and walk the long way around," he said, confidently taking my arm.

On the station platform, he kissed me. It was a *fabulous* kiss, an unexpected birthday gift. I was powerless to stop him getting on the train with me; we were still kissing when it arrived. But on the walk home, I warned him, "Look, you can come in for literally five minutes, but I really do have to do something special, on my own, at midnight."

"I want to watch," he said, lasciviously, squeezing my waist. I rolled my eyes.

"It's not something sexy," I assured him. Adding, "You'll think I'm weird."

"I already think you're weird," he said, and I fell silent, battling the voices that tried to echo his judgement.

"I don't care," I said quietly, finally... firmly.

When we got into the house, I retrieved my cupcake from the refrigerator and put it on a plate with a knife. Then I got my Tiffany's bag from my room and placed it next to the plated cupcake on the coffee table. I sat on the couch in front of them. Tim sat opposite me in a chair.

I really, *really* didn't care what he thought.

I carefully unwrapped and then opened the Tiffany's box and took out my beautiful silver bracelet. It was a struggle to fasten it around my wrist with one hand.

Tim got up, saying, "Can I help you?"

"No," I said firmly. "I have to do this myself." He sat back down promptly and I looked up at him and smiled, explaining, "I have to be able to do it myself. You won't be here to do it at other times."

"You don't know that for sure."

But I did. Suddenly I knew I wouldn't see this man again. I didn't need to. This had been nice, but anything more could lead to the beginnings of a relationship and that was firmly off the cards until... well, I had no idea when.

I finally got the bracelet secured around my wrist. I rested my left wrist in my right hand, looked down and said, to myself, "I promise to love you and take care of you, forever."

Then I looked up at Tim, who was staring at me, bemused.

"Can I offer you a piece of cake?"

"It's a little small," he said. The look on his face told me that, while he may have thought me weird, he was also somewhat entertained, and possibly even impressed, by my little ceremony.

"It was meant for one," I said, cutting the little cake into two pieces. "But I'm very happy to share it with you." I bit into my half and passed him the plate. He took a bite and then got up and came and sat beside me.

"Can I have a little piece of *you*, now?" he cooed, nibbling my ear.

I couldn't resist one more make-out session before detangling myself from Tim's long, sexy arms, sitting up and saying, "Look, I'm really sorry, but I have to ask you to leave now. I do need to be on my own this birthday." Taking in his crestfallen look I realized I had never, ever in my life, *ever*, asked a man to leave. I had always let them take control. "You have my number," I reassured him. (I'd

242

given it to him in the bar earlier, before he'd insisted on accompanying me home.) "And I would love to go out with you sometime," I lied. "Soon," I reassured him as I coaxed him off the couch.

"Okay," he muttered.

I pulled him towards the front door and as I opened it, he stepped towards me, pulling me in for a final kiss. I let him kiss me once more, for a few seconds, before gently but firmly pushing him away.

"I'll call you soon," he said.

"Okay," I said, waving at him and shutting the door, not caring in the least whether he did or didn't.

And then I realized something.

He never actually wished me a happy birthday.

And I saw what I was to him with absolute clarity. I was an intriguing challenge, but I meant nothing to him. And why *should* I mean anything to him? He had known me for less than three hours. And I thought of all the men in the past, and how much of myself I had given them before knowing if they valued me, before *letting* them find out if there was something to value. Maybe I'd never felt particularly valuable before.

I went to bed with an unfamiliar feeling inside me. As I drifted off to sleep, I wondered what it was. When I woke up on my birthday morning, I knew, and I named it...

Self-worth.

I spent my birthday as I'd planned to: with myself.

First I took the Gold Line Downtown and paid my very first visit to MOCA (the Museum of Contemporary Art). I'm picky about modern art, but Rothko, Jasper Johns and

Cy Twombly all particularly intrigue me, and I discovered even more artists I liked. I walked over to Little Tokyo for lunch and then headed back to Pershing Square, via a ride on the Angels Flight, the tiny funicular railway between Olive and Hill. I discovered the historic Biltmore Hotel and took a little wander through its historic corridors, marvelling at the murals, before heading back up to Pasadena.

I spent the afternoon at the Norton Simon museum and immersed myself in the vast collection of Impressionist paintings, the pleasing abstract shapes of Kandinsky, Giacometti's stick people, the Degas bronzes, and the sculpture garden that boasted a couple of Henry Moore's and a cast of Rodin's *The Thinker*. I was enchanted by the whole collection in this museum, and voted it a clear winner over its rival, The Getty Center.

After my late, rather boozy night the previous evening, I opted to spend my actual birthday night at home. I cooked myself dinner and watched *The Shawshank Redemption* (to prove to myself that real Tim Robbins was far superior to my recent suitor).

Fake Tim called twice. I didn't answer or call him back. He still didn't wish me a happy birthday. He just asked me to call him because he couldn't wait to see me again.

The week after my birthday I hosted "book club" in the back yard. This was a monthly event that the Mad Cat Lady had always hosted at her house. Her wonderful friends, Natalie included, decided there was no reason for it to stop or move location while she was away. It was traditionally a "pot luck", with everyone bringing an assortment of things to eat and drink, so it really was no effort at all.

"Book club", I discovered, was a misnomer. This dynamic

group of fabulous, interesting women had started meeting two years earlier. The original remit was, of course, to read books and discuss them. But no one ever had any time to read, and when they did, they had much more interesting things to discuss when they saw each other anyway, so it became a monthly catch up. No reading required.

Those ladies became my new crew. I began meeting up with some of them for coffees and lunches. None of them worked in the Entertainment Industry. They had normal jobs. They lived in places I'd never heard of but grew to love, like La Cañada and Altadena.

As for the Entertainment Industry, I finally got a response from the producers. They liked my new draft very much. Could I just tweak a few more *minor* things?

I didn't respond immediately.

I was busy.

What made my new life so different and interesting was that I had taken to the streets. We get so addicted to our cars in L.A. To be fair, even with my new love of public transport, I had to admit that it was a little sporadic; it can't take you *everywhere* you want to go, the city is too spread out, but a little bit of effort is all it takes to have a different experience, and it's worth it.

Once I was moving around on rail, bus and foot, I saw all kinds of new landscapes. Some, incredibly beautiful (like the inside of the Biltmore Hotel) and some desperately harrowing, like Skid Row, a place I'd only previously seen depicted in *The Soloist*. I wandered through it by accident one day, after a visit to the Los Angeles Public Library (another eye-opening delight) as I made my way over to the

Japanese American National Museum. I stood and listened to a man playing the most beautiful flamenco music on a Spanish guitar on the corner of San Pedro and 3rd Street. Where was Steve Lopez now? Why had only one man been rescued? What would become of all the others?

Hollywood… or rather the Entertainment Industry… had given me tunnel vision. When I started looking outside of my world, my limited experience of L.A., I was mesmerised by the fascinating, diverse world I found. For a place that is so often written off as being "shallow", it had depths that were profoundly moving.

About two weeks after I'd met him, and after I'd assumed he'd gone away because I hadn't returned his calls (it usually made me go away when I didn't get my calls returned by a guy I liked), Tim showed up at my door, drunk, at 11pm on a Friday night.

I didn't know whether he'd come in a cab, via the metro and on foot, or (I dreaded to think) had driven in that state, but I was a little freaked out he'd remembered my address.

I didn't let him in.

"Why won't you return my calls? I like you. You're hot!"

"Thank you," I said. "But I'm sorry, I'm not dating anyone right now."

"Come oooonnnnn…" he whined through the little peephole window in the door that I'd opened. "Let me in. I'm not going to do anything you don't want me to do."

"I don't *want* you to come in," I said firmly.

"You're funny with the dating yourself thing," he said in a softer tone, "but you're just lonely. We'd be good together; I know it. I knew it the minute I saw you."

Why was this sounding strangely familiar?

246

"I'm sorry," I said again. "Please go. I'm going to move away from the door now. You have to go."

"Whyyyy?" he called out, desperately. "I'm a nice guy. I'm one of the good guys."

"I know," I said. Now… wait for it – I was cracking up before I said it. *"It's not you, it's me!"*

I couldn't stand up I was suddenly laughing so hard at the irony. I sank to the floor, doubled up with the giggles, but doing my best not to make too much noise. Tim went incredibly quiet as I shook in semi-silent mirth.

I thought he might have gone and then a little voice called through the door.

"Are you laughing at me?"

Well, that just set me off again. I was weeping with the effort not to laugh and pee myself simultaneously as I tried to assure him, "It's. Not. You. It's. *Me!*"

I was gone again. Doubled up. Holding my sides.

Never in all my born days did I think I'd hear myself saying those five little words that had haunted me when used in the opposite direction.

I have no idea how long I lay there once I'd stopped laughing, but as soon as I was sure I couldn't hear a sound outside, I tentatively opened the door.

Tim had gone. I never saw or heard from him again.

A bruised ego will only push so far.

I started to feel settled for the first time in forever. I enjoyed the company of my friends, old and new, but I continued to do plenty of things by myself. I took myself to movies, to dinner sometimes, to art galleries and concerts. I started to *enjoy* doing things by myself. Not because it was *better* than doing them with someone else (it was just different) but because it was liberating. If I didn't *have* to have someone to do things with, there was no limit to what I could do. And I didn't have to put up with someone who wasn't right for me for fear of having no one to do things with.

And sometimes it was nice, just to watch a movie and drive home *thinking* about it, instead of analysing it to death with someone and disagreeing on what the ending actually meant. Maybe the ending isn't meant to *mean* anything. Maybe the story just ends.

I was experiencing true love; true *self* love.

For the very first time in my life, my happiness did not depend on being in a relationship, or how I fared in the field *between* relationships, it depended entirely on how I treated *myself*. I had spent my whole life defining myself by the men I had in my life, or hoped to have in my life, always assuming that the right one would make me happiest. But now I knew, only I could make myself happy. That came first, regardless of the person or people I had in my life, regardless of where I lived.

Wait.

Was that last bit technically true? Granted I'd moved to a different *part* of L.A. but I was a short car ride from everything I knew, everything that was familiar. Everywhere I called home. But it wasn't home. London was home. Or was it?

All of a sudden, I didn't know where home was. And, surprisingly, that thought didn't scare me; it *excited* me. Maybe, I thought, I could live *anywhere*.

My aunt once told me that true love meant you didn't care where you lived as long as you were with the person you loved.

"I could have lived in a shoe box. Or on the moon," she said, "as long as my husband was with me." If I truly loved myself, could I live anywhere with me? Could I leave the familiar? Could I give up my routines, my industry... my crazy little gold car?

You know me well enough now. I might be a clinger, but I am a girl who will always take a challenge.

"But I don't want to go among mad people," Alice remarked.

"Oh, you can't help that," said the Cat: "we're all mad here. I'm mad. You're mad."

"How do you know I'm mad?" said Alice.

"You must be," said the Cat, "or you wouldn't have come here."

Alice's Adventures in Wonderland,
Chapter 6

LEWIS CARROLL

Alice got up and ran off…

Alice's Adventures in Wonderland,
Chapter 12

LEWIS CARROLL

CHAPTER TWELVE

The Girl Who Ran Off

Was I the girl who loved herself?

You can't have failed to notice that I am a little in love with L.A., but I would be the first to admit that it's all a little mad and a *lot* addictive. All that sunshine, the beaches and the mountains, endless fresh produce, beautiful people, the cultural diversity, easy parking (except at Trader Joe's), and the – physical and emotional – space to reinvent yourself, any time you want… discounting the gang crime issue, (which, granted, is a big issue in pockets of the city) it's a couple of droughts and forest fires off perfection.

But it is a bubble. It's so big that, when you're in it you can't see out of it.

Unless you make a conscious effort to browse the Internet for world news regularly, or keep your radio tuned to NPR and your TV set to CNN, it's all too easy to forget that there's a whole world going on beyond the Los Angeles city limits.

The longer you stay, the harder it is to leave. You talk yourself out of it. *Will I survive out there in the wild? What if there's nowhere like Trader Joe's? They might call with the offer for my screenplay next week. I have to be in town in case I get the audition for that movie. Where will I find ripe avocados? Maybe I won't leave yet. I'll just stay a little bit longer.*

Every time I'd ever left L.A. after a period of working there, it was because something dragged me away: a boyfriend who didn't want to live there, or a job I had to go to in London.

This time, it was going to be *my* choice.

I needed to take off my training wheels and find out if whatever I'd discovered about living with myself and loving myself would stick out there in the big wide world, without my L.A. cushion for comfort. It was going to be a wrench, especially as I was beginning to feel so calm and settled, but I knew L.A. was too much of a safety harness; I was too seeped in my L.A. identity, even if I had shifted from "Hollywood Writer" to "White Girl in Gangland".

But I definitely didn't want to go back to London. I could imagine how quickly all the work I'd done would be undermined if I fell back into my old life (minus the ex) back there. I definitely wasn't ready to face up to and overcome my London identity, which was wrapped up in who I was as a girlfriend, daughter and sister.

No, I *really* needed to test myself, away from any ghosts of the past.

So I bought a ticket to somewhere I'd never been before.

I spent the next few weeks organizing my life. I reached out to a British publisher I'd once worked for and they were delighted to hear from me. They had a book-editing job for me. Obviously I could do it on the road.

And maybe that was what gave me the guts to stand up to the Hollywood Machine that had yanked my chain for two years. I called the producers and did something that would have previously been unthinkable to me. I told them I wasn't doing any more changes on the script. I said they could take it to the network in its current state, or we could call it a day.

They said they'd get back to me.

I'm still waiting.

I contacted the Mad Cat Lady to check her return date hadn't changed. I'd booked my ticket with it in mind but wanted to make sure there was no change on her end, in case we needed to find cat care cover. But she was on track to return as planned.

She was excited for me, and even offered me space in her basement storage area if I wanted to leave some of my things, instead of shipping them back to London. I thanked her but declined. I wanted a clean break.

I got to work on sorting through my possessions, giving away as much as I could and boxing up the rest to ship to the storage facility in London that housed my half of the contents of the flat I'd lived in with the ex.

I bought a massive backpack from Target… along with other travelling essentials.

I had a lovely farewell dinner with Natalie and Stella at our favourite pizza place in Eagle Rock. I told Stella I was going on a big adventure. She told me I was brave.

"So if you ever get scared, just remember you were *so* brave to go on an adventure, you're not really allowed to be scared. So *then* you will feel even more brave, like *super* brave."

I remembered the guy from the salsa club, who'd said, "You brave lady."

A stranger had seen me clearer than I could see myself.

Now I was getting life lessons from a 6-year-old. Well, lucky me.

I had a real wobble one afternoon, just after taking another bag of clothes to Goodwill. What was I thinking? Why did I think I could go off on my own to somewhere I'd never been before? What if this newfound strength and confidence didn't last? What would I do if I couldn't take care of myself when the chips were down? How long did I think I could do this for? What would I do afterwards? Where would I go? Was this just a thinly veiled excuse to avoid learning to live with myself and get settled? Was I actually just sabotaging my happiness, running away the minute I'd found a great place to live in and a bunch of really nice new friends?

Why had I snubbed Tim?

What if he was *the one*?

Whoa! I caught myself in that trap of habitual thinking. *That* was what could undermine my strength. I could pick apart my good work any time I wanted if I wasn't careful.

The day before my departure I had to say goodbye to one more place. I drove over to Silver Lake and parked up on Sunset so I could walk up the hill.

When I got up to the house, the side gate was open.

"Hello," I called out.

There was no answer so I walked up the little stone steps. The door to the treehouse was closed and it looked like no one was home. I turned and walked out onto the little terrace. It was exactly as I'd remembered it. It hadn't

256

been that many months since I'd lived there but it somehow felt like a lifetime ago… because I'd changed so much. This place, now, was a reminder of the girl I'd been, the girl who had hated herself, the girl who had come face to face with her inner demons, the girl who had fallen apart, the girl who had given up. And now I was the girl who had figured some things out, the girl who had taken herself dancing and to New York and to gangland. Soon I was going to be the girl who went on an adventure into the unknown.

Was I the girl who loved herself?

I sat down on the bench with my legs crossed under me, rested the backs of my hands on my knees, and closed my eyes.

Immediately I felt warm all over. I breathed in and out, slowly. I had no idea how long I sat there but this time I knew I wasn't asleep because I could feel my cheeks aching… from smiling.

"I love you," I whispered, effortlessly.

And then, before I knew it, I'd said all my goodbyes. I'd sold my car, and rented one for my last few days. I'd had all my farewell drinks and lunches. I'd packed my last box and handed them all over to the shipping company. I'd forwarded my mail.

I drove myself to LAX. I'd had plenty of offers but I needed to do this bit alone. I had paid the supplemental fee to return my rental car to the company's airport location.

I tried to stay calm as I checked my bag and went through security. I'd left L.A. countless times, but always to go back to London, and usually knowing exactly when I'd return. I knew nothing now. I didn't know what to expect where I was going. I didn't know how long I'd stay there.

The next chapter of my life was a blank page.

Before I knew it, my plane was taking off. It was a crystal clear day in December and as we climbed into the sky I looked down at the beach where my crazy journey had begun.

The Pacific Ocean was the deepest blue I'd ever seen. The crests of the waves twinkled in the sunlight.

I kept my face pressed to the window, not wanting to lose sight of L.A. as it got smaller and smaller, and suddenly I thought of the words my dear friend T— had once used, what she'd said to the world when she'd had to put on hold her crazy New York life of juggling a high profile job and a hectic social life, to have her first baby.

I spoke those words now, as I looked down at the diminishing city of angels that I loved so much. I squished my face right onto the window and whispered, though my tears, "Just gotta go do something... I'll be right back."

—there's a special providence in the fall of a sparrow. If it be now, 'tis not to come: if it be not to come, it will be now: if it be not now: yet it will come; the readiness is all—

Hamlet,
Act 5, Scene 2
WILLIAM SHAKESPEARE

I didn't set out to write a book, I set out to figure out why my relationships always ended in heartbreak. But over time, whenever I told people my story, they didn't say, "Wow, that would make a great book." They didn't even say, "Oh, you *must* write that as a book." They all, without exception, said, "*Please* write that book!"

I toyed with the idea and started a few times, but couldn't face going through with it. It was intense enough living it once. But it kept nagging me and I eventually wrote a lengthy first draft that took a great deal of sweat and tears (no blood, I assure you). I quickly banished that draft to a well-concealed folder in the depths of my hard drive, swearing never to look at it again.

Then, one day, something told me it was the right time. *The readiness is all.*

I opened that nasty, banished draft, realized I had finally acquired the skills to tell the story the way I felt it needed to be told, and started rewriting the whole thing.

As I wrote the manuscript that you've just read (unless you've skipped to the end), an incredible thing happened. I thought I was done – on an emotional and developmental level – with this particular passage of time. But, to my surprise, I think I learned more about myself, found more value from my experiences, in the *telling* of this story than I ever did in the *living* of it.

I think that's because the pure, naked truth always lies deeper than we realize, or can admit and accept.

The nineteenth-century painting *La Vérité sortant du puits armée de son martinet pour châtier l'humanité* (English translation: Truth emerging from the well with her whip to punish humanity) by the French painter Jean-Léon Gérôme shows a naked woman, representing Truth, who has been thrown down a well by "liars and actors" (as explained in the title he originally gave an earlier version of the painting). She is shown climbing out of the well with her whip in hand, ready to wreak vengeance on those who banished her.

When I look at this painting, I don't see the *whip* as her means of punishing humanity, I see her exposed *nakedness* as the real weapon. People don't want to see the truth, so the very sight of her will terrify them. The whip, in my opinion, is actually her means of fighting them off when they try to throw her back into the well, the means with which *she will fight and conquer shame.*

We all live with the Naked Truth about who we really are buried inside us. And we spend most of our lives throwing her back down the well when she tries to climb out. We cannot face our shame, so we cover it, bury it, disguise it, do anything but look at it... let alone allow anyone *else* to look at it!

But we cannot progress, on a personal level or as a species, if we let the "liars and actors" take centre stage and make us hide behind our shame, so much so that we can't even name our shame: *shame.*

Even Franklin D. Roosevelt couldn't name it. When he

262

said, "The only thing we have to fear is fear itself," in his first inaugural address in March 1933, he defined that fear as the "nameless, unreasoning, unjustified terror which paralyzes needed efforts to convert retreat into advance."

What was he talking about? *Shame*! Americans were ashamed of the greed that had led to the economic crisis of the Great Depression, ashamed of how many lives had been lost in their oxymoronically named "civil war" and the gross injustices that had befallen the most vulnerable in society for years… ashamed of their lust for power, and powerless to admit it.

Until we face our naked truths and whip away the deafening catcalls of shame, we will only ever run around in circles falling down wells and failing to retain any self love in our leaky buckets.

It's not easy.

I'm still trying to face the ugliest truths and fix the last few holes in my bucket.

And that's one of the reasons I finally told this story: to face the truth of it, without shame. Obviously I haven't documented every single thing that happened to me during the course of this year (some things are way too boring and others are simply too depressing to relive) but, as I promised, I have told you the *truth of my journey*… the emotional beats of my story.

Whoever you are, wherever you reside, whatever stage of life you are at, you have a story. And like every fingerprint, every story is unique. But we all share something in common. We share the conundrum that is the human experience. Because to exist is to be in conflict, all the time, between what we know and what we don't know. Our stories are unfolding every second of every day. The truth is only known *after* the fact; we can't know it in advance. I don't know what will happen in the next moment, or the moment after that, or in any future moment until it's happened. I have a pretty good idea, but I don't know for *certain*. And no matter how much I try to "be in the present" and "live in the now" *not knowing* how the story ends drives me *crazy*.

And it drives you crazy, too.

Don't try to deny it!

So we do our best to trust that the story will end well, that our loved ones will not suffer too much, that we will be able to pay our bills, and that we will have the courage to step up to the plate when the time comes. Because we will *all* be called to step up to the plate one day, and do the most heroic thing… *face our truth*.

Maybe you've been there. Maybe you don't want to believe me, but there will come a time when you'll know what I'm talking about, or if you look back on your life now you'll recognize the moment you had that call. Did you answer it? Or is it still calling you? Trust me, it won't stop!

When I sat on a beach, in Santa Monica, one seemingly insignificant afternoon, and closed my eyes, and asked – I don't know who or what – to pick me up and lift me out of the despair I felt, I was asked to step up to the plate. I was asked to face my truth.

I didn't know then that the journey I needed to embark on would change my life so profoundly, and possibly help to change others'.

I cannot tell you how scared I was, how much I wanted to ignore that call. I wanted to write it off as a momentary lapse in sanity. "Date" myself? What a ridiculous notion. I didn't want to do it. I didn't what to do it *at all*. I knew I'd have to face all kinds of crap. But I made myself do it. I felt the fear and did it anyway. And over the years, as I've spoken about this story, about my journey, people have told me how grateful they are... because, they say, they really "needed" to hear *this* story.

Yes, of course there's more! Getting on that plane and leaving L.A. was only the first step along the next leg of my journey, parts of which were even worse than anything I'd experienced before. For example, I soon reached the point where I was genuinely worried that I'd rendered myself incapable of connecting, intimately, with another person ever again, that I'd isolated myself and eschewed romantic love to the point of being terrified of it.

But that's a whole other story.

So let's leave me now, 37,000 feet above the Pacific Ocean, hurtling at speeds of over 500mph towards a day I would never experience (only because I'm about to cross the International Date Line, nothing more dramatic, don't worry) and the day after that, which would be the very first day of the rest of my life.

As every new day is.

The End
(of the Beginning)

265

Lightning Source UK Ltd.
Milton Keynes UK
UKHW020653310520
364051UK00002B/25/J

9 781999 347710